NAG HAMMADI STUDIES
VOLUME XVI

NAG HAMMADI STUDIES

EDITED BY

MARTIN KRAUSE - JAMES M. ROBINSON
FREDERIK WISSE

IN CONJUNCTION WITH

ALEXANDER BÖHLIG - JEAN DORESSE - SØREN GIVERSEN
HANS JONAS - RODOLPHE KASSER - PAHOR LABIB
GEORGE W. MACRAE - JACQUES-É. MÉNARD
TORGNY SÄVE-SÖDERBERGH
R. McL. WILSON - JAN ZANDEE

XVI

GENERAL EDITOR OF THE COPTIC GNOSTIC LIBRARY
JAMES M. ROBINSON

LEIDEN
E. J. BRILL
1981

THE COPTIC GNOSTIC LIBRARY

EDITED WITH ENGLISH TRANSLATION, INTRODUCTION AND NOTES

published under the auspices of

THE INSTITUTE FOR ANTIQUITY AND CHRISTIANITY

NAG HAMMADI CODICES

GREEK AND COPTIC PAPYRI

FROM THE

CARTONNAGE OF THE COVERS

EDITED BY

J. W. B. BARNS†, G. M. BROWNE
AND J. C. SHELTON

LEIDEN

E. J. BRILL

1981

ISBN 90 04 06277 7

PRINTED IN THE NETHERLANDS

CONTENTS

FOREWORD

"The Coptic Gnostic Library" is a complete edition of the Coptic
Gnostic codices: Nag Hammadi Codices I-XIII, Papyrus Berolinensis 8502, the Askew Codex and the Bruce Codex. It includes a
critical text with English translations to each codex and tractate,
notes, and indices. Its aim is to present these texts in a uniform
edition that will promptly follow the appearance of *The Facsimile
Edition of the Nag Hammadi Codices* and that can be a basis for
more detailed technical and interpretive investigations. Further
studies of this sort are expected to appear in the monograph series
Nag Hammadi Studies of which The Coptic Gnostic Library is a
part.

This edition is a project of the Institute for Antiquity and
Christianity, Claremont, California. The translation team consists
of Harold W. Attridge, John W. B. Barns†, Hans-Gebhard Bethge,
Alexander Böhlig, James Brashler, G. M. Browne, Roger A. Bullard,
Peter A. Dirkse, Joseph A. Gibbons, Søren Giversen, Charles W.
Hedrick, Wesley W. Isenberg, T. O. Lambdin, Bentley Layton,
Violet MacDermot, George W. MacRae, Dieter Mueller†, William
R. Murdock, Douglas M. Parrott, Birger A. Pearson, Malcolm L.
Peel, James M. Robinson, William C. Robinson, Jr., William R.
Schoedel, John C. Shelton, John H. Sieber, John D. Turner,
Francis E. Williams, R. McL. Wilson, Orval S. Wintermute,
Frederik Wisse and Jan Zandee.

The volumes and editors of The Coptic Gnostic Library are as
follows: *Nag Hammadi Codex I*, volume editor Harold W. Attridge;
*Nag Hammadi Codices II, 1, III, 1 and IV, 1 with Papyrus Beroli-
nensis 8502, 2: The Apocryphon of John*, edited by Frederik Wisse;
Nag Hammadi Codices II, 2-7 and III, 5, volume editor Bentley
Layton; *Nag Hammadi Codices III, 2 and IV, 2: The Gospel of the
Egyptians (The Holy Book of the Great Invisible Spirit)*, edited by
Alexander Böhlig and Frederik Wisse in cooperation with Pahor
Labib, Nag Hammadi Studies 4, 1975; *Nag Hammadi Codices III,
3-4 and V, 1 with Papyrus Berolinensis 8502, 3: Eugnostos the
Blessed and the Wisdom of Jesus Christ*, edited by Douglas M.
Parrott; *Nag Hammadi Codices V, 2-5 and VI with Papyrus
Berolinensis 8502, 1 and 4*, volume editor Douglas M. Parrott, Nag

Hammadi Studies 11, 1979; *Nag Hammadi Codex VII*, volume
editor Frederik Wisse; *Nag Hammadi Codex VIII*, edited by
Bentley Layton, John Sieber and Frederik Wisse: *Nag Hammadi
Codices IX and X*, volume editor Birger A. Pearson; *Nag Hammadi
Codices XI, XII and XIII*, volume editor Charles W. Hedrick;
*Nag Hammadi Codices: Greek and Coptic Papyri from the Cartonnage
of the Covers*, edited by J. W. B. Barns†, G. M. Browne and John C.
Shelton; *Pistis Sophia*, text edited by Carl Schmidt, translation and
notes by Violet MacDermot, volume editor R. McL. Wilson, Nag
Hammadi Studies 9, 1978; *The Books of Jeu and the Untitled Text
in the Bruce Codex*, edited by Carl Schmidt, translation and notes
by Violet MacDermot, volume editor R. McL. Wilson, 1978, Nag
Hammadi Studies 13, 1978. Thus, as now envisaged, the full scope
of the edition is thirteen volumes.

John W. B. Barns happened into the Library of the Coptic
Museum on 16 January 1971 while the Technical Sub-Committee
of the International Committee for the Nag Hammadi Codices was
at work there. He was invited to return to advise concerning
papyrological matters, which he did on 21 January 1971, at which
time it was agreed that he would prepare a critical edition of the
cartonnage. On 5 May 1971 he was supplied with photographs of
the parts of the cartonnage of Codex VII that were already exposed
to view. On 21 May 1971 he reported a date for the hand of text 66
(VII, 6ᶜ) to the first quarter of the Fourth Century. In September
1971 photographs became available of the bulk of the cartonnage of
Codex VII, which by then had been separated by Abd el-Moeiz
Shaheen, Sub-Director of the Centre for the Study and Conservation
of Antiquities of the Egyptian Antiquities Organisation. On the
basis of these photographs Barns provided on 31 October 1971
preliminary datings of text 63 (VII, 2ᶜ) to 342 A.D. and of text 64
(VII, 3ᶜ) to 339 A.D., suggesting a resultant date for the library
"only a few years later." Barns' preliminary results were published
in "The International Committee for the Nag Hammadi Codices:
A Progress Report," *New Testament Studies* 18 (1972), 240, and
The Facsimile Edition of the Nag Hammadi Codices: Codex VII
(Leyden: E. J. Brill, 1972), p. ix. Rodolphe Kasser had already
identified the Genesis fragments from Codex VII on 21 December
1970, and published them in "Fragments du livre biblique de la
Genèse cachés dans la reliure d'un codex gnostique," *Le Muséon* 85
(1972), 65-89.

In December 1971 Abd el-Moeiz Shaheen also separated carton-nage of Codices IV, V and VIII. Photographs were then supplied to Barns, who worked on all this material in Cairo during the fourth session of the Technical Sub-Committee in December 1972. The cartonnage of Codex I had meanwhile been made available by Jean Doresse on 29 August 1972 at Claremont, California. On 20 October 1972 photographs of what was exposed to view were sent to Barns for inclusion in his work. On 4 September 1973 Barns supplied a preliminary photographic mock-up of the cartonnage for *The Facsimile Edition of the Nag Hammadi Codices*, in terms of which the cartonnage was conserved in Cairo in September 1973. Barns then prepared a preliminary report on the content of the cartonnage thus far available, "Greek and Coptic Papyri from the Covers of the Nag Hammadi Codices," posthumously published in *Essays on the Nag Hammadi Texts: In Honour of Pahor Labib* (Leyden: E. J. Brill, 1975), pp. 9-17. On 10 December 1973, the same day on which Barns mailed his manuscript, E. G. Turner examined the cartonnage of Codex I during a visit to Claremont; I reported his views to Barns on 17 December, as did Turner himself before Christmas. But the sudden lamentable death of Barns on 23 January 1974 prevented him from incorporating the work of Turner in his own preliminary report, for which reason Turner provided a "Comment" printed with Barns' essay (pp. 17-18).

Early in 1974 Eileen C. Barns was kind enough to make available the files of her husband so that his work could be made available to a successor who would carry it through to completion. I am indebted to G. M. Browne for consenting to assume this responsi-bility, and to John C. Shelton, who subsequently assumed responsi-bility from Browne for the Greek material. Late in 1974 Anton Fackelmann removed the cartonnage from the covers of Codices VI, IX and XI, and on 28-31 October 1973 and 28 March 1975 the cartonnage was removed from the cover of Codex I. Browne was able to examine the cartonnage of Codex I in Washington, D.C. in April 1974 and in Claremont in June 1975, and the cartonnage in the Coptic Museum in July 1974 and December 1976. He has supplied information already published in the *Facsimile Edition: Codex I* (1977), pp. xv and xvii; *Codex IV* (1975), p. ix; *Codex V* (1975), p. xi; *Codex VIII* (1976), p. xi; and, together with John C. Shelton, *Cartonnage* (1979), pp. xv, xvii, xix and xxi.

The team research of the project has been supported primarily through the Institute for Antiquity and Christianity by the National Endowment for the Humanities, the American Philosophical Society, the John Simon Guggenheim Memorial Foundation, and Claremont Graduate School; and through the American Research Center in Egypt by the Smithsonian Institution. Members of the project have participated in the preparatory work of the Technical Sub-Committee of the International Committee for the Nag Hammadi Codices, which has been done at the Coptic Museum in Cairo under the sponsorship of the Arab Republic of Egypt and UNESCO. Without such generous support and such mutual cooperation of all parties concerned this edition could not have been prepared. Therefore we wish to express our sincere gratitude to all who have been involved.

A special word of thanks is due to the Egyptian and UNESCO officials through whose assistance the work has been carried on: Gamal Mokhtar, President until 1977 of the Egyptian Antiquities Organization, our gracious and able host in Egypt; Pahor Labib, Director Emeritus, Victor Girgis, Director until 1977, and Munir Basta, currently Director of the Coptic Museum, who together have guided the work on the manuscript material; Samiha Abd el-Shaheed, Curator for Manuscripts at the Coptic Museum, who is personally responsible for the codices and was constantly by our side in the library of the Coptic Museum; and, at UNESCO, N. Bammate, Deputy Assistant Director General for the Social Sciences, Human Sciences and Culture until 1978, who has guided the UNESCO planning since its beginning, and Dina Zeidan, specialist in the Arab Program of the Division of Cultural Studies, who has always proved ready with gracious assistance and helpful advice.

We also wish to acknowledge our great indebtedness to the two directors of Brill during the years in which this volume was in preparation, F. C. Wieder, Jr., Director Emeritus, and T. A. Edridge, whose role as Director has been cut short by his untimely death. Without the support of such outstanding leaders in the field of scholarly publication not only this volume, but the whole series of Nag Hammadi Studies, indeed The Facsimile Edition of the Nag Hammadi Codices, would not have been possible.

JAMES M. ROBINSON

CONCORDANCE WITH THE PLATES OF THE
FACSIMILE EDITION

The inventory numbers (to the left) are used in the conservation of the papyri and the plates of *The Facsimile Edition of the Nag Hammadi Codices: Cartonnage* (Leiden, 1979); the numeration of the texts (to the right) is that used in the present volume. Coptic texts are distinguished by the prefix C.

Codex I		Codex V (cont.)		Codex VII (cont.)		Codex VII (cont.)	
1^c	1	14^c	30	3^c	64	80^c	133
2^c	2	15^c	31	4^c	65	89^c-93^c	C 2
3^c-4^c	3	16^c	32	5^c-6^c	66	94^c-96^c	C 4/C 5
5^c-6^c	4	17^c	33	7^c	67	97^c	C 6
7^c-9^c	5	18^c	34	8^c	68	98^c	C 7
10^c	6	19^c	35	9^c	69	99^c	C 6 or C 7
11^c-12^c	7	20^c	36	10^c	70	100^c	C 3
13^c	C 1	21^c	37	11^c	71	101^c	C 8b
14^c-17^c	8	22^c	38	12^c	72	103^c	C 8c
19^c	9	23^c	39	13^c-14^c	73	104^c	C 8a
20^c	10	24^c	40	15^c	74	105^c	C 8d
22^c	11	25^c	41	16^c	75	106^c	100
25^c	12	26^c	42	17^c	76	107^c	101
26^c	13	35^c	43	18^c-19^c	77	108^c	102
28^c	14			20^c-21^c	78	109^c	103
33^c-34^c	15	**Codex VI**		22^c	98	110^c	99
		1^c	44a/45a	23^c-24^c	79	111^c	C 9
Codex IV		2^c	44b/45b	25^c	83	112^c	104
1^c	16	3^c	44c	26^c	84	113^c	105
2^c	17	4^c	46/47	27^c-29^c	80	114^c	106
3^c	18	5^c-6^c	44d-e	30^c	81	115^c	C 10
4^c-5^c	19	7^c	48	31^c	82	117^c	C 11
6^c	20	8^c	49	32^c	86	118^c	C 12
21^c	21	9^c	50/51	33^c	85	120^c	C 13
		11^c	52	34^c	87	121^c	108
Codex V		12^c-13^c	53	35^c	88	122^c	109
1^c	22a	14^c	54	36^c	89	124^c	110
2^c	22b/23a	15^c	55	37^c	90	125^c	111
3^c	22c/23b	16^c	56	38^c	91	126^c	C 14
4^c	22d/23c	17^c	57	39^c	92	127^c	112
5^c-8^c	22e-h	18^c	58/59	40^c	93	128^c	113
9^c	24	19^c	60	41^c	94	129^c	114
10^c	25/26	25^c	61	42^c	95	130^c	124
11^c	22i/23d			43^c	96	134^c	115
12^c	27	**Codex VII**		44^c	97	135^c	116
13^c	28/29	1^c	62	51^c	107	136^c	117
		2^c	63				

Codex VII (cont.)		Codex VII (cont.)		Codex VIII		Codex IX	
137ᶜ	118	148ᶜ	130	1ᶜ-12ᶜ, 15ᶜ,		1ᶜ	146
138ᶜ	119	149ᶜ	131	19ᶜ	143	2ᶜ	147
139ᶜ	120	150ᶜ	132	20ᶜ-27ᶜ	144	3ᶜ	148
140ᶜ	121	152ᶜ	134	28ᶜ-29ᶜ	145	4ᶜ	149
141ᶜ	122	153ᶜ	135	30ᶜ-36ᶜ	C 18	5ᶜ	150
142ᶜ	123	154ᶜ	136	37ᶜ-40ᶜ	C 17	6ᶜ	151
143ᶜ	125	155ᶜ	137	41ᶜ-45ᶜ	C 16	7ᶜ	152
144ᶜ	126	156ᶜ	138	46ᶜ	C 15	Codex XI	
145ᶜ	127	157ᶜ	139	58ᶜ-59ᶜ	C 19	1ᶜ	153
146ᶜ	128	158ᶜ	140				
147ᶜ	129	159ᶜ	141				
		160ᶜ	142				

LIST OF PAPYRI ARRANGED BY CODEX

TABLE OF GREEK PAPYRI

NOTE ON EDITORIAL PRACTICE AND LIST OF ABBREVIATIONS

The editorial signs employed in this volume are those in common use: square brackets [ ] indicate a lacuna, parentheses ( ) resolution of an abbreviation or symbol, angular brackets < > a mistaken omission in the original, double square brackets ⟦ ⟧ a deletion by the scribe, and high strokes ' ' superlinear additions, but not letters raised to mark an abbreviation. Dots within brackets, or numerals within brackets, indicate the approximate number of letters lost in a lacuna; dots outside brackets indicate illegible letters, and dots under letters indicate uncertain readings. Punctuation and, in the Greek texts, accents, breathing marks, and iotas subscript have been added by the editors. Faults of spelling and grammar have been pointed out in a critical apparatus or discussed in textual notes when they could not be conveniently indicated in the text itself. A horizontal arrow → indicates that the writing on a given papyrus surface runs parallel to the fibers, a vertical arrow ↓ that it runs perpendicular to the fibers.

As regards supralineation in the Coptic texts, printing requirements have necessitated a certain amount of deviation from absolutely accurate reproduction: strokes between two letters on the original are placed over the second in the transcript, and long lines over three letters are centered over the second. For the precise placement of the supralinear stroke, the reader should consult *The Facsimile Edition of the Nag Hammadi Codices: Cartonnage* (Leiden, 1979).

Individual dates have not been assigned to the Coptic texts, but it is likely that they were written approximately in the first half of the fourth century A.D. (cf. Introd. p. 5, n. 10).

The reader is reminded that although some consultation of the originals was possible, the greater part of the editorial work was based on photographs; in particular, the surviving editor of the Greek texts has not seen the papyri and in doubtful cases has often necessarily relied upon the Brussels MS (for which see the list of abbreviations below). Details of the transcripts should therefore be judged with due caution.

In addition to the standard abbreviations of editions of papyri and scholarly journals, we have used the following shortened references:

Blass-Debrunner-Rehkopf, *NTGrammatik* = F. Blass, A. Debrunner, *Grammatik des neutestamentlichen Griechisch*. Bearbeitet von F. Rehkopf. 14th ed., Göttingen 1976.

Brussels MS = A typescript including preliminary transcripts of the texts in this volume with the exception of those from the cover of Codex VI, occasionally with translations and some commentary, prepared by G. M. Browne on the basis of material left by J. W. B. Barns and partly controlled by Browne on the originals. Its readings have generally been followed unless a photograph showed a clearly preferable alternative.

Crum, *Dict.* = W. E. Crum, *A Coptic Dictionary*. Oxford 1939.

CSEL = *Corpus Scriptorum Ecclesiasticorum Latinorum*. 1866ff.

Du Cange = Charles Du Fresne Sieur Du Cange, *Glossarium ad Scriptores Mediae et Infimae Graecitatis*. Lyon 1688, reprint Graz 1958.

Gignac, Phonology = F. T. Gignac, *A Grammar of the Greek Papyri of the Roman and Byzantine Periods*. Vol. I, *Phonology*. Milan 1976. *Testi e documenti per lo studio dell' antichità* 55.

Halkin = *Sancti Pachomii Vitae Graecae*, ediderunt Hagiographi Bollandiani ex recensione Francisci Halkin S. I. Brussels 1932.

Kasser, Compléments = R. Kasser, *Compléments au Dictionnaire copte de Crum*. Cairo 1964. *Bibliothèque d'études coptes* 7.

Kühner-Gerth = R. Kühner, B. Gerth, *Ausführliche Grammatik der griechischen Sprache*. 2. Teil, *Satzlehre*. 3rd. ed., Hannover and Leipzig 1898-1904.

Lampe, *PGL* = G. W. H. Lampe, *A Patristic Greek Lexicon*. Oxford 1961.

Mandilaras, *The Verb* = B. G. Mandilaras, *The Verb in the Greek Non-Literary Papyri*. Athens 1973.

Mayser = E. Mayser, *Grammatik der griechischen Papyri aus der Ptolemäerzeit*. Leipzig 1906ff.

Naldini, *Cristianesimo* = M. Naldini, *Il Cristianesimo in Egitto. Lettere private nei papiri dei secoli II-IV*. Florence 1968.

NB = F. Preisigke, *Namenbuch enthaltend alle griechischen, lateinischen, ägyptischen, hebräischen, arabischen und sonstigen semitischen und nicht-semitischen Menschennamen, soweit sie in griechischen Urkunden (Papyri, Inschriften, Mumienschilder usw.) Ägyptens sich vorfinden*. Heidelberg 1922.

Oertel, *Liturgie* = F. Oertel, *Die Liturgie. Studien zur ptolemäischen und kaiserlichen Verwaltung Ägyptens*. Leipzig 1917; reprint Aalen 1965.

Onomasticon = D. Foraboschi, *Onomasticon alterum papyrologicum. Supplemento al Namenbuch di F. Preisigke*. Milan 1967. *Testi e documenti per lo studio dell' antichità* 16.

Pape = W. Pape, G. Benseler, *Wörterbuch der griechischen Eigennamen*. 3rd. ed. Braunschweig 1911; reprint Graz 1959.

PG = *Patrologiae cursus completus, Series Graeca*, ed. J. P. Migne. 1857ff.

PL = *Patrologiae cursus completus, Series Latina*, ed. J. P. Migne. 1878ff.

Prel. Rep. = J. W. B. Barns, "Greek and Coptic Papyri from the Covers of the Nag Hammadi Codices: a Preliminary Report", in *Essays on the Nag Hammadi Codices in Honour of Pahor Labib*, ed. M. Krause (Leiden 1975) 9-17, with an addendum by E. G. Turner pp. 17f.

WB = F. Preisigke, *Wörterbuch der griechischen Papyrusurkunden mit Einschluss der griechischen Inschriften, Aufschriften, Ostraka, Mumienschilder usw. aus Ägypten.* Berlin 1925ff.

INTRODUCTION

It was probably in December of 1945 that a party of Egyptian *sabakh*-diggers discovered under the sheltering side of a fallen boulder the sealed jar which when broken open was found to contain the manuscripts that are now known as the Nag Hammadi Library. Reportedly the jar was discovered together with a corpse (though not from an ancient burial) on a bed of something resembling charcoal, but this was not confirmed by excavations on or near the site thirty years later in December 1975. However that may be, one of the party, Mohammed Ali, took the manuscripts back to his home in al-Qasr, the ancient Chenoboskia, some three and a half miles from the place of discovery near the tiny village Hamra Dom. There he deposited them among straw that was to be used as fuel for a clay oven in the courtyard, and some of the material was consequently later burned; but much the greater part was saved and eventually came into possession of the Coptic Museum in Old Cairo, where it is kept today.[1]

The manuscripts proved to contain an immensely valuable collection of Coptic religious writings, many of which had been previously quite unknown, and which for the most part strongly reflect Gnostic teachings. In addition they contained the fragments of Greek and Coptic papyri which are published in the present volume. These had been used simply as scrap paper: the twelve codices are bound in leather, and eight of these leather covers are strengthened with a layer of used papyrus. The late J. W. B. Barns undertook to edit this so-called cartonnage in 1971. The following survey of texts is intended to complete and update the preliminary report on the documents which Barns had prepared before his death in 1974 and which was published posthumously the following

---

[1] The paragraph above is based on James M. Robinson's "From the Cliff to Cairo: The Story of the Discovery and the Middlemen of the Nag Hammadi Codices", of which the author kindly sent me a manuscript copy. The most informative account known to me which had been published at the time of this writing is by the same scholar in *The Nag Hammadi Library in English* (Leiden, 1977) 21-3.

year,[2] as well as to correct it in some respects. In particular the
question as to whether the documents found in the codex covers
support the theory that the codices themselves once belonged to
the library of a Pachomian monastery requires new consideration.

This question was answered in the positive by Barns in his
Preliminary Report, but it will be seen below that evidence for
monasticism in general in these papers is less frequent than was
supposed in that work,[3] and there are no texts in which a specifically
Pachomian background comes plainly to the fore (cf. pp. 5-11). It
should be emphasized, however, that the nature of the cartonnage,
though of use for determining the approximate date and place at
which the codices were bound, is of very questionable value for
determining their ownership.[4]

The covers that contained papyrus cartonnage are the following:

Codex I (**1-15**; **C1**). Two contracts, an account that mentions
weavers' goods, a mutilated private letter, and several fragments
of unidentifiable nature. The first of the contracts (**1**) requires
special mention, as it has previously been reported to indicate a
"monastic background; it mentions a μονή and a *proestōs*, and the
name of Chenoboskion occurs in it".[5] This view was reached on the

---

[2] "Greek and Coptic Papyri from the Covers of the Nag Hammadi
Codices: a Preliminary Report", in *Essays on the Nag Hammadi Codices in
Honour of Pahor Labib*, ed. Martin Krause (Leiden, 1975) 9-17, with an
addendum by E. G. Turner pp. 17f. Henceforth *Prel. Rep.* It should be
noted that the last of the material did not become available for study until
its detachment from the cover in 1975.

[3] ". . . most of the contents of [Codex] VII, and some of I and VIII,
indicate a monastic background" (*Prel. Rep.* p. 12). Evidence for monasticism
is now limited to some of the correspondence in Codex VII, discussed below
pp. 5-11.

[4] "Now it seems unlikely that the writing of the codices and their binding
should have been the work of two different establishments; and even more unlikely that the waste papyrus used to pack and strengthen the covers should
have had no connection with the binders" (*Prel. Rep.* 11-12). Clearly the
persons who strengthened the covers had access to the materials they used
for that purpose, but this does not get us very far. I see no prima facie
connection between scribes and bookbinders, nor between those two parties
and the owners of the codices. A monastery might, of course, use its own
discarded documents for binding its manuscripts, but it might also have used
material from any convenient source for this purpose, or have acquired
volumes that were already bound. Conversely, secular or heretical parties
could have used the cast-offs of an orthodox religious body.

[5] *Prel. Rep.* 12.

basis of photographs made before the fragments had been completely freed from the cover. E. G. Turner found on the original that κώμης should be read in place of μονῆς, and warned that *proestos* can have other meanings than that of the head of a monastic organization.[6] Later a further portion of the document was found and the fragments were rearranged following a suggestion of Professor Turner. It is now clear that *proestos* in the text refers to the chairman of a guild of oil-workers who were contracting to supply oil for the municipal supplies of Diospolis Parva, here called "Diospolis near Chenoboskia" (l. 4). So far as can be determined, therefore, all texts in this cover are purely secular. The hands indicate dates in the late third or first half of the fourth century A.D.

Codex IV (16-21). Fragments of accounts mentioning wine, wheat, and barley in such large quantities that taxation or military rations are probably involved. They were presumably written in some government office in the fourth century.

Codex V (22-43). The two longest documents, 22 and 23 (front and back of the same papyrus), are parts of official accounts concerned with an area at least as large as the two procuratorships of the Thebaid; they would be of great interest if they were better preserved. Of numerous other fragments in the cover, the great majority appear likewise to be official accounts, though 28 may be part of a contract and the nature of 31 is doubtful: one might think of a contract, petition, or report. The natural source of such texts would again be a government office, possibly that of the *praeses Thebaidos*. The location of his seat of office at the time our texts were written is unfortunately not known: near the end of the fourth century it was Antinoopolis, but there is some reason to think that it may have been Hermopolis earlier (see P. Beatty Panop. p. xx; A. K. Bowman, *BASP* 15, 1978, pp. 33, 36-7). As 22 and 23 were written while the Thebaid was divided into two ἐπιτροπαί, those texts can be dated roughly between 298 and 323 A.D. All the papyri in the cover were written in the late third or early fourth century.

Codex VI (44-61). For the most part name lists and accounts; again taxation suggests itself as the purpose. 53 is a document of a different type, presumably a petition, report, or fragment of cor-

---

[6] *Prel. Rep.* 17-8.

respondence addressed to a strategus or epistrategus; the same
choice of officials recurs in **56**. The papyri may have come from the
same source as those in the covers of Codices IV and V, and were
written at about the same time.

Codex VII (**62-142**; **C2-C14**). This is by far the richest of the
covers in point of view of the number and condition of the documents preserved. It is not easy to summarize briefly.

Religious literature: **C2**, some fragments of Genesis, and possibly
C3, an exhortation to virtue which could be part of a homily or an
epistle. A suggestion that Pachomius, the traditional founder of
coenobitic monasticism, may have been the author [7] is not presently
subject to proof or refutation. I do not know whether a fourth-
century monastery would be more or less likely than other groups
or individuals to use bits of Holy Scripture (**C2**) to strengthen a
book cover. Such use would, of course, have the effect of physically
preserving the writing, but it is more than doubtful that that was
the intention in this case.

Contracts: **62**, remnants of a sale of some kind. It was previously
dated to the consulship of Domitius Zenophilus (A.D. 333) or
Tettius Facundus (A.D. 336),[8] but it is argued in the introduction
to the text below (p. 52) that the reign of Aurelian or the rebel
Domitius Domitianus, or the consulship of Flavius Domitius
Leontius (A.D. 344), are more probable. **63** is a loan of wheat,
dated to 20 November 341. The signature of the illiterate debtor
was written by a former municipal magistrate, but we do not know
of what city.[9] **64** is another loan of wheat, drawn up between a
resident of a previously unknown village Techthy in the Little
Diopolite nome and a former magistrate of Dendyra. If the debtor
took the contract back home with him after paying the loan, it was
in Techthy or thereabout when it came into the hands of the bookbinders. Date 21 November 346. The debtor, one Aurelius Comes,
was tentatively identified in *Prel. Rep.* p. 12 as a presbyter who is
one of the writers of our letter **77**. If so, he does not mention his
position (which would be odd) or did not have it yet; but it is by

---

[7] *Prel. Rep.* 15.

[8] *Prel. Rep.* 12.

[9] It was erroneously reported in *Prel. Rep.* p. 12 that the debtor of this
contract, Aurelius Psenetymis, is "almost certainly" to be identified with a
man, evidently a monk, named in one of the letters in this cover. In fact
the name Psenetymis does not occur again among these papers.

no means certain that the presbyter was in fact named Comes (cf. **64**.4 n., **77**.16 n.). **65** is a deed of surety, addressed to the chairman of some municipal council. Dated to October of A.D. 348, it provides a terminus a quo for the cover of this codex.

Private letters: whenever the religious faith of the correspondents of the many letters found in this cover can be determined, it is invariably Christian. Particularly welcome are some of the earliest references yet found to monks and the light shed on their daily lives.[10] There were important coenobitic monasteries of the Pachomian order at Pabau and Chenoboskia, respectively about 5½ and 3½ miles from the place where these texts were discovered. These were Pachomius' second and third monasteries; the foundation dates are uncertain, but in any case they were later than the first establishment at Tabennese (*c.* 320-5 A.D.) and were flourishing by the time of Pachomius' death (probably 346). Our letters were written in the early to mid fourth century and so are roughly contemporaneous with the growth of Pachomian monasticism. As it has been suggested that the Nag Hammadi codices themselves, despite their generally heretical and sometimes non-Christian nature, once belonged to the library of one of these orthodox organizations,[11] it is of some interest to enquire whether the material

---

[10] The earliest datable reference to an Egyptian monk is P. Collect. Youtie II 77.15 from A.D. 324, recently studied by E. A. Judge, "The Earliest Use of Monachos for 'Monk' (P. Coll. Youtie 77) and the Origins of Monasticism", *Jahrbuch für Antike und Christentum* 20 (1977) 72-89. The letters in the Nag Hammadi covers are not dated, but on palaeographical grounds they are not likely to be more than about thirty years later than that at the outside.

[11] The argument in *Prel. Rep.* 12ff. is as follows: there are no traces of heresy or heterodoxy in the cartonnage documents; the findspot of the texts was near the monastery of Chenoboskia; and "since it is hardly conceivable that there would have been more than one orthodox monastic organization simultaneously operating in the same place, we should be justified in concluding, even without further evidence, that the Nag Hammadi material came from a Pachomian monastery" (p. 13); further evidence is then forthcoming in the form of texts which mention names identical with those of persons known to have been active in the Pachomian organization, including perhaps Pachomius himself.—To this it can be said that there is no more evidence for orthodox than for heterodox beliefs in the documents, as none reveals the shading of its author's Christianity; none of the personal identifications are (to this writer at least) convincing; and the few texts which give some indication as to the way of life of the persons concerned are difficult or impossible to reconcile with Pachomianism. This last point is, however,

used in the covers reflects a Pachomian background. The following discussion will be largely concerned with this question.[12]

It should be stated at once that there is not enough evidence to settle this on Christological grounds. The letters do include a number of Biblical echoes and pious sentiments, but these are all dogmatically quite neutral and could have been written by virtually anyone whose views were recognizably Christian.[13] One general consideration weighs against a Pachomian attribution, but it is hard to say how heavily—the great majority of the correspondence

---

very problematic, as our sources on classical Pachomianism may be misinformed or deliberately idealized, or may represent a stage of development later than that of the papyri; at the same time, the papyri themselves must not be used to correct impressions from other sources unless it can be proved that the papyri are Pachomian. In the discussion of individual texts below I shall take possession of money and other private property, interest in secular concerns, and apparently free contact with the daily world, in particular with women, as speaking against a Pachomian background.

[12] It may be as well to mention at this point some other possibilities; it will be recalled that Pachomius himself made provision for the reception of visiting monks who did not follow his order (Halkin pp. 24-5, *PL* 23.73, *PG* 40.949). Meletian monasteries had been established by A.D. 334 (P. Jews 1913). A series of interesting fourth-century letters to an anchorite is printed in P. Jews. 1923-9. Most of the early papyrological attestations of monks apparently refer to the class which Jerome called *remnuoth* (*Ep.* 22.34 in *CSEL* 54 and *PL* 23); see Judge, *art. cit.* in n. 10 above. As such a monk could own land and other property (cf. for example the sales of dwellings in SB I 5174-5) and was obliged by some means to support himself, his contact with the world must have been immeasurably greater than that of the possession-less Pachomian within his cloister walls, and so it is only natural that we should hear more of him than of the Pachomian coenobite in documentary papyri. A considerable body of late correspondence evidently concerning *remnuoth* has been published in P. Epiph. II. Cf. also the Christian fellowships discussed by E. Wipszycka, "Les confréries dans la vie religieuse de l'Égypte chrétienne", *Proceedings of the Twelfth International Congress of Papyrology* (Toronto, 1970 = ASP VII) 511-25, esp. 519f.

[13] Another view was expressed in *Prel. Rep.* pp. 12-3: "Nowhere do we find any suggestion of heresy or heterodoxy; indeed, this seems ruled out by a passage in one letter which speaks of the commendation (συνέστησεν) of an individual to a group of the brethren by 'our father [the holy ?] bishop'." The letter referred to is our **77**, but it shows only that certain presbyters respected their bishop; we should have to know the latter's religious leanings to pass judgment on their orthodoxy. The use of such terms as ἀδελφός, πατήρ, μοναχός, and πρεσβύτερος in the letters is likewise orthodologically uninformative: they can all be found similarly used, for example, in the Meletian report on misdoings by the followers of Athanasius in P. Jews 1914.

is in Greek, whereas the Pachomian monasteries of the area were
predominantly Coptic.

There are only two letters which beyond all reasonable doubt
came from or into the hands of monks, **72** and **C8**. **72** was sent by
a woman to Σανσνῶτι καὶ Πσάτος μοναχοῖς: she asks them to try to
find some chaff for her asses and let her know how much it costs
per waggonload. Here one can deny a Pachomian background with
considerable assurance: a normal member of a Pachomian organization would not have been in a position to fulfill this request and it
is almost unthinkable that he would have received correspondence
from a woman—or indeed a man—on such a subject, as the point
of Pachomian coenobitic life was to avoid just such secular concerns. The monks here may have belonged to another order, or the
text may date to a period before Pachomianism had taken on its
classical form, but it seems most probable that they are further
examples of Jerome's unorganized *remnuoth* (see n. 12).[14] One of the
men, Sansnos, may be identical with a presbyter of the same name
discussed below, pp. 8-9.

C8, a letter from a monk, includes a greeting to "all the brothers"
(frag. a, l. 8) and refers to someone called "my father Sansnos"
(a 14) and "Apa Sansnos". If that should be the Sansnos of **72**,
the brethren can hardly have been Pachomian, but the name was
very common.[15]

The possibility of a monastic background arises in several other
letters as well, although monks are not specifically mentioned in
them.

67 includes a request to have some wheat transported to a
μονάχιον and stored in a σιρός there. The word μονάχιον has not
occurred before, but it should indicate a monks' dwelling of some
kind; a σιρός was sometimes an underground bin, sometimes

---

[14] It may be significant that **72** is addressed to *two* monks; the Epiphanius
correspondence alone includes 26 more such letters. The editor writes: "In
some cases . . . the relation was that of teacher and disciple . . . in others
merely that of two anchorites of like standing, who share a cave or hut"
(P. Epiph. I p. 138).

[15] **C8** is the letter which was described in *Prel. Rep.* p. 15 as "seem[ing]
to compare the growth of the particular community to which it was addressed
to that of a grain of mustard seed", but this view was based on a false placing
of the fragments; see **C8** a 14 n.

simply a large vessel used for storing grain.[16] Many examples of privately-owned σιροί are known; [17] the μονάχιον need not have been very large to have possessed one.

We are not told the positions of the correspondents in **67** or the reason for transporting the grain, but the writer speaks of "the brothers who are with you and those with me" (l. 12). Though the phrase is of itself indecisive, it seems natural in this context to suppose that two groups of monks, or at least religious fellowships of some sort, are meant. Nothing points specifically to Pachomian life.

77 and **78** are both letters from presbyters to a fellow presbyter named Sansnos. He may be identical with the monk Sansnos of **72**, though there is no reason to think so apart from the name.[18] In addition there are five letters written to a Sansnos whose position is not identified: **68, 73, 75, 76, C5**. We see him asked to intervene to protect a tenant from harassment by his landlord and to obtain some chaff for the writer (**68**; cf. n. 21), to turn over five artabs of wheat to a "brother" (**75**), and, if it is the same man, to put off buying some wheat and to attend to some financial affairs (**C5**). As the request to obtain some chaff in **68** is reminiscent of that in **72**, where Sansnos is called a monk, there is some reason to think that the same person is meant. Indeed, the presence of so many letters addressed to Sansnos gives the impression of a small archive of correspondence received, though I am doubtful whether it is really one archive or at least two. There is further a letter in very un-educated Greek written *by* a Sansnos to one Aphrodisios (**69**), scolding the latter for having failed to send food for some "lads"

---

[16] For σιροί as underground bins cf. F. Luckhard, *Das Privathaus im ptolemäischen und römischen Ägypten* (Giessen, 1914) 83; Pliny, *NH* XVIII 306; and see the excavation report in P. Epiph. I p. 42 with other remarks on the storage of grain by monks ibid. p. 146. The σιροί of P. Giss. Univ.-Bibl. II 17, on the other hand, must be vessels of some kind, as they are located in an upper room; the editor cites Hesychius for the definition πίθος.

[17] E.g., P. Mich. V 195; P. Teb. III. 2 851.37 and 82; 852.98; 959.11.

[18] It should perhaps be pointed out in this connection that according to the *Vitae* there were no presbyters in early Pachomian organizations: ὅταν χρεία ἦν προσφορᾶς, μετεκαλεῖτο πρεσβύτερόν τινα τῶν ἔγγιστα ἐκκλησιῶν . . . οὐ γὰρ ἦν ἐν αὐτοῖς τις γενόμενος ἐν καταστάσει κλήρου ἐκκλησιαστικοῦ (Halkin p. 16). But at a later time ecclesiastics were permitted, provided they claimed no special privileges for themselves (*ibid.* p. 17), and there are in any case other grounds for doubting that the monk Sansnos was Pachomian (p. 7).

(παιδία, possibly slaves) and informing him of some matters concerning sheep and goats. It would be very surprising if this text were to be found in company with letters that the same man had received. I much doubt that it refers to the monk and/or presbyter.[19]

Of the remaining Greek letters of this codex which are well enough preserved to give some idea of their content, one, **71**, is addressed to two presbyters, asking them to buy two skins for the writer: he sends them two artabs of dates as part payment in advance, and will pay the balance when he learns how much it is. The other letters (**66, 70, 74, 79-81**) are evidently purely secular and show no involvement with monasticism.

The Coptic letters, of which two have already been mentioned (**C8** p. 7, **C5** immediately above), show in general a greater tendency to express Christian sentiments and less concern with worldly affairs than the Greek texts.

C4 is a pious and tender letter to Aphrodisi(os), who may be called an ascetic (l. 25 n.) and is recovering from a recent illness.[20] Aphrodisios is also the name of the recipient of a Greek letter from some Sansnos (**69**): the scolding, impatient tone of the Greek letter contrasts strongly with the respectful, even reverent tone of the Coptic one, but there is no particular reason to believe that the same Aphrodisios is involved.

The Aphrodisios of **C4** plainly lived in a religious fellowship of some sort, and apparently his correspondent lived in another one. The writer speaks of a "brother" named Sourous (l. 16). A Sourous was the first head that we know of in the Pachomian monastery at Pachnoum. This may be the same man, but if so it is perhaps odd that he is not called "father".

---

[19] This doubt considerably weakens the case for believing that Sansnos and his associates, as the parties responsible for the tending of sheep and goats, were also in charge of leather-work and the production of the covers of the Nag Hammadi codices, as was argued in *Prel. Rep.* 14. The same text does, however, mention a Sansnos "the shepherd" who is obviously not the same as the writer of the letter (**69**.17, 20). If he could be shown to be the monk/presbyter (who is not otherwise connected with animals), then the reasoning of *Prel. Rep.* would gain some support; so far as we know, however, the man was simply a shepherd.

[20] The improvement in Aphrodisios' health did not last long if one may judge from **C5**, which he himself wrote later and in which he declares that he does not know whether he will live or die (ll. 9-10). The Epiphanius correspondence also includes numerous reports of illness among monks; cf. P. Epiph. I pp. 163f.

Aphrodisios later used the other side of the papyrus to write a letter of his own to Sansnos (**C5**). This is almost wholly concerned with business affairs: Sansnos is to put off making a purchase of wheat, to collect some money, and to pay part of it out again. One can think of positions even within Pachomian life in which such matters would have to be handled in the interests of the monastery, but in that case one would have expected the instructions to have been given verbally; and there is no indication that Aphrodisios was acting for a monastery rather than for himself.

C6 is part of a letter from Papnoute (Papnutius) to Pahome (Pachomius). Virtually nothing of its content is still discernible: the great interest of the text lies in the mutilated address on the back, which it is possible to understand as "Deliver it (the letter) to my prophet and father Pachomius, from Papnutius". If this should be correct, the addressee could very well be the great Pachomius himself; moreover, Papnutius might also be historically identifiable, as the first general oeconome of all the monasteries was named Papnutius.[21] Since both he and Pachomius resided in the same monastery at Pabau they must normally have communicated with each other verbally, but of course special circumstances could have occasioned a letter, and in any case the identification of Pachomius is not dependent on that of his correspondent. However, the phrase which one would have partly to restore, ⲡⲁⲡⲣ[ⲟ]ⲫⲏⲧ [ⲏⲥ] ⲛ̄ⲉⲓⲱⲧ (for the . ⲁⲡⲣ[.] . ⲏⲧ[. .]⁻ⲉⲓⲱⲧ of the text), does

---

[21] A Greek letter, **68**, may further be relevant: it contains a request to "make Petros, who is harassing brother Appianus through Papnutius and his people because of the rents, hold off for a few days" (ll. 3-6). Rent collection would obviously fall within the sphere of competence of an οἰκονόμος, but one must question whether the general oeconome of the Pachomian monasteries can be meant here. The word for rent used, ἐκφόρια, is normally used of rent in kind, and strongly implies that Appianus had leased some farm land from the Petros named. This Petros is evidently Papnutius' superior, since he can use the latter as his agent. If Papnutius was the Pachomian oeconome, then the land must have been monastery property, and Petros must have held a very high position indeed—abbot of one of the cloisters, perhaps. But there seems to be no evidence that the early Pachomian monasteries owned land which they leased out: the monks appear rather to have done the work themselves. As the picture of Pachomian monks harassing slow-paying tenants is in any case bizarre, one would prefer to have more evidence before identifying this man as Pachomius' oeconome. There is no real indication as to whether he is the writer of **C6**.

not appear to be attested elsewhere.[22] Pachomius was among the commonest of Egyptian names. As there are otherwise no clear traces of the Pachomian order in these texts, one may be sceptical about the identification of the man here.

C8 has been discussed above, p. 7. The remaining Coptic fragments from the codex are too small to give a clear idea of their content.

Finally, Codex VII contained a Greek *account*, secular so far as one can tell (**82**).

In summary, it may be said that Codex VII presents us with a very mixed assortment of texts ranging from secular contracts to monastic letters and bits of Scripture. It is hard to think of a satisfactory single source for such a variety of documents except a town rubbish heap—which may indeed have been the direct source of all the papyri the bookbinders used.

Codex VIII (**143-5**; **C15-C19**). A series of ordinances, probably imperial, would be of major importance if the text were better preserved (**143-4**). The office or offices in which the tax documents in other covers were presumably produced would very likely have also had an interest in such ordinances. In addition there are letters in Greek (**145**) and Coptic (**C15-C18**, possibly also **C19**), all too mutilated for their content to be determined.

Codex IX (**146-52**). The nature of **149-51** is unclear. The remainder appear to be fragments of tax accounts similar to those in Codex VI and may have come from the same source.

Codex XI (**153**). The only text in this codex of which the nature can be determined is a fragmentary letter written by an inhabitant of Chenoboskia.

On the basis of place names mentioned in the cartonnage it may be concluded that at least Codices I, V, VII, and XI were bound using material from the general neighborhood of the place where the codices were found. A terminus a quo for Codex VII can safely be set: it was bound during or after October of A.D. 348 (**65**). There are no certain traces of classical Pachomian monasticism in the cartonnage.

JOHN C. SHELTON

---

[22] The reverse phrase, however, ⲡⲁⲉⲓⲱⲧ ⲙ̄ⲡⲣⲟⲫⲏⲧⲏⲥ, is common enough; see **C6** *verso* 6f., n.

PART ONE

THE GREEK PAPYRI

BY

J. W. B. BARNS† AND JOHN C. SHELTON

CODEX I

1. UNDERTAKING BY OIL-WORKERS

I 1ᶜ   7.5 × 11.5 cm.   late 3rd/early 4th cent.

The oil-workers of a village in the Little Diopolite nome, having previously agreed to supply oils for the εὐθένεια of the nome capital, agree in the present text to continue and expand their responsibilities in this enterprise. Virtually no details are preserved, but the existence of such an agreement presupposes that the workers involved were organized into some form of corporate unity: see in general M. San Nicolò, *Ägyptisches Vereinswesen zur Zeit der Ptolemäer und Römer* (2nd ed. Munich 1972 = *Münchener Beiträge* 2/I + 2/II), with oil-workers' guilds in particular pp. 78-80. The name of the party with whom the agreement was made is lost at the beginning of the text. A eutheniarch would be the obvious guess.

The papyrus has been mentioned by John Barns, *Prel. Rep.* p. 12, and partly transcribed by E. G. Turner, *ibid.* 17-8; cf. Introd. pp. 2-3. Dark traces which appear above l. 1 in the *Facsimile Edition* plate 3 are not ink. The back is blank.

—   —   —   —   —   —   —   —   —

→   ] . . Διοσ

                 ] . ωμων

        ] . [   ] Πεκύσιος

[. . . . . ἀπ]ὸ τῆς (αὐτῆς) Διὸς πόλ(εως) περὶ Χηνοβ(όσκια)

5   [. . . . . .]των ἐλαιουργῶν κώμης

    [. . . . . .] τοῦ (αὐτοῦ) νομοῦ δι(ὰ) Ηδεμυδρα

    [. . . . .]ος προεστῶτος ἀπὸ [τῆ]ς (αὐτῆς) κώμης

                χαίρειν.

[ἐπε]ὶ ἔδοξεν ὥστε κοινῇ ἡμᾶς παρα-

10 [σχε]ῖν τῇ εὐθενείᾳ τῆς πόλεως ἔλαια

    [. . . .] . . . ια, κατὰ ταὐτὰ ὁμολογοῦμεν

    [. . . . .]ιω καὶ αὐθαιρέτῳ γνώμῃ ἐπιγνῶ-

    [ναι . . . . . .] πάντα τὰ διαφέροντα τῇ αὐτῇ

    [. . . . .] καὶ τὰ ἄλλα ἐπιτάγματα καὶ μὴ

15 [. . . . . . .] ἐκ τῶν πρὸς ἀλλήλους συνθηκῶν

    [. . . .] . πίας δι' ἁπαξαπλῶ[ς] . [

    [. . . . .] . θα . . . [

—   —   —   —   —   —   —   —   —

(l. 4)   '. . . from the same Diospolis near Chenoboskia, (all of
us?) oil-workers from the village . . . of the same nome, through
Hedemyras (?) son of NN, chairman, from the same village,
greeting. Seeing that it was decided that we would jointly supply
. . . oils for the food supply of the city, we in like manner agree of
our own . . . and free will to take upon ourselves all the responsibilities of the same (public function) and (to carry out) the other
orders and not to (repudiate?) the contracts of . . . with one another
(on any pretext) whatever . . .'

1-5   The structure of these lines was: addressee(s) in the dative,
now lost; names of oil-workers in the nominative, acting through
their guild chairman, greeting.

1   The traces before Διοσ are too slight to permit a reading;
syntactically attractive would be ἀ]πὸ Διὸς | πόλεως or κ]αὶ Δῖος,
Διόσ|κορος, Διοσ|κουρίδης or the like.

4   Διὸς πόλ(εως) περὶ Χηνοβ(όσκια): Diospolis Parva. The expression has not been found before, but it is comparable to Διοσπολίτου περὶ Χηνοβ( ) used for the Little Diopolite nome in P. Ant.
I 32.2 and 32, where Χηνοβ( ) should be expanded as here on the
basis of the accusative Χηνοβόσκ[ι]α in SB X 10277.16 and the
dative Χηνοβοσκίοις in W. Chr. 447.14 and M. Chr. 87.39. *RE* III
2285 cites from literary sources two variants, Χηνοβοσκία and
Χηνοβόσκιον, to which Χηνοβοσκεῖα can now be added from Halkin's
edition of the Greek life of Pachomius; none of these have so far
appeared in papyri (the last of them would, however, be unrecog-
nizable in accentless texts, as the interchange of ι and ει is too
common to be decisive even if Χηνοβοσκεια should one day be found.
It is not a possible alternative to Χηνοβόσκ[ι]α in SB X 10277.16).
A further form, Χηνοβόσκιοι (*WB* III 339), is simply a false abstrac-
tion from the dative in M. Chr. 87.39. Concerning the town cf.
Alexander Polyhistor apud Steph. Byz. s.v. Χηνοβοσκία: ''ἀντικρὺ
δὲ τοῦ Διοσπολίτου [νομοῦ] Χηνοβόσκιον, μηδὲν εἰς τὴν προσηγορίαν
ἐμφέρουσα· νομὰς γὰρ χηνῶν οὐκ ἂν ἴδοι τις, ὑπερβάλλουσαν δὲ τὴν περὶ
κροκοδείλους σπουδήν.''

5   Probably πάν]των at the beginning; apparently not τῶν
λοι]πῶν or ἄλ]λων.

6   τοῦ (αὐτοῦ) νομοῦ: i.e., the Little Diopolite.

Ηδεμυδρα: context requires a personal name, or the beginning of
one. No name similar to this is elsewhere attested, but the ono-

mastics of this region are poorly known, and this volume in general contains an accordingly high proportion of additions to our name lists. A more familiar phrase would be ἡ δὲ μιχρά, but I see no way of fitting it into context without assuming major errors in the drafting of the text.

7 προεστῶτος: guild chairman. Cf. e.g. BGU IV 1028.8 for a προεστὼς κλειδοποιῶν, l. 25 π. χαλκέων, P. Oxy. X 1275.8 π. αὐλητῶν καὶ μουσικῶν. All these examples are taken from WB III 148.

10 εὐθενείᾳ: for bibliography see P. Köln I 55.3/4 n., P. Oxy. XXXVIII 2854 introd.

11 -ια is presumably the end of an adjective modifying ἔλαια.

12]ιω: one expects [ἑκουσ]ίᾳ καὶ αὐθαιρέτῳ γνώμῃ, but the Brussels MS reports a clear ω. After ω the papyrus is damaged: one letter may have been lost. If so, [ἑκουσ]ίω[ς] would be tempting. [ἀμετανοή]τῳ cannot be read.

12-3 Perhaps ἐπιγνῶ|[ναι ὁμοίως.

14 χρεία alone would be too short for the lacuna at the beginning of the line, δημοσίᾳ χρείᾳ too long unless abbreviated. λειτουργίᾳ or ἐπιμελείᾳ would do.

15 The lacuna is likely to have held a word for "abandon" or "neglect"; e.g., ἐκστῆναι.

16 E.g., δι' ἁπαξαπλῶς [μ]η[δεμιᾶς προφάσεως.

2. FRAGMENT OF A SALE (?)

I 2ᶜ   14 × 10 cm.   late 3rd/early 4th cent.

Line 12 shows that this document involved a sale, but it follows unconventional formulas and is in places so badly rubbed that in the lack of parallels little is intelligible. Possibly it is not a sale as such, but a legal settlement of some kind which included a sale as one of its terms. Revision on the original would be desirable. The back is blank.

--- --- --- --- --- --- --- ---

→   ] . . . [. . . . .]μ[
2   ] . . ου . . . . [   ] . . νται προπ[
3   ]υϛλουσ . ει . . . [. . . . .] τῆς γε ἀπὸ τοῦ (αὐτοῦ) ζ′
                                      εὐ[τ]υ[χῶς
4   -το]ς ἔτους . . μαν[. . . .] ἐὰν δὲ ἐπέλθω ἢ μὴ καὶ [
5   ] . . . . . σερια[. . ἐ]πὶ δὲ τῆς αἰτήσεως τὸ ἀντίγρ[αφον

6   ] . ε[.] . [.] . νειαυ[.] . [.] τοῦ καὶ 'Ερμείνου Εὐδαίμονος
                    α . [
7   ]χου . . . [. .] ἀπὸ τῶν νομων ἐπιγραφην[
8   ἀ]ναγρα(   ) ὁ Τριφρονῶς παρόντι καὶ εὐδ[οκοῦντι
9   ] . . . . . . ὁ καὶ Κοπρεᾶς Εὐδ[αίμο]νος ε[
10   ἀ]ναγρ(   ) Πιμέλι τῷ καὶ Κοπρεᾷ. κυρία [
11   ] περὶ δὲ τοῦ ταῦτα ὀρθῶς καλῶς γεγενῆ[σθαι
12   (m. 2)]ων ἀπέσχον τὴν τιμὴν καὶ ἐμ[μενῶ

3-4   The obvious supplement is εὐ[τ]υ[χῶς εἰσιόντο]ς ἔτους, but
it is also thinkable that the lacuna was much larger than this. The
point of division between the lines is in any case uncertain.

7   ἐπιγραφήν or ἐπιγραφῆν[αι. Context does not show whether the
preceding word means "nomes", "laws", or "pastures".

8   Τριφρονῶς: I have retained the reading of the Brussels MS, as I
can offer no certain correction from the plate. The line as a whole
would construe as ἀ]ναγρα(φῆναι) Τρίφρολι ὡς παρόντι καὶ εὐδ[οκοῦντι,
"to be registered to Triphrolis as if he were present and giving his
approval". Neither Triphrolis nor Triphronos is very satisfactory
as a name, however. Τριφρόνιμος would be formed on a more familiar
pattern. None of the three is in the *NB* or *Onomasticon*.

9   At the beginning probably Πιμέλις, the same individual as in
the next line, but I cannot confirm this from the plate. Πιμέλις is
not in the *NB* or *Onomasticon*; cf. Μέλι, Μέλιος, etc.

10-11   The minimal supplement is κυρία [ἡ πρᾶσις.

11   After γεγενῆ[σθαι supply ἐπερωτηθεὶς ὡμολόγησα, possibly
abbreviated.

12   E.g., ἐμ[μενῶ πᾶσι τοῖς προκειμένοις. It is unclear whether the
contract ended at this point or the subscriptions of further parties
followed.

3.   PRIVATE ACCOUNT

I 3ᶜ + 4ᶜ   (a) 2.5 × 6.8 cm.   late 3rd/early 4th cent.
                 (b) 8.8 × 10 cm.

Two non-contiguous fragments of a badly mutilated private
account, to some degree concerned with weaving and weavers'
products. Judging from the alignment of the fibers and the ar-
rangement of the lines, it seems probable that frag. (a) preserves
portions of the same lines the ends of which are to be found in frag. (b)

col. i, and the text below is printed on that assumption. The last
line preserved of each column is probably the last that was written.
Revision on the original would be desirable. The back is blank.

Col. i

— — — — — — — — — —

→
```
                               ] . ονω . (  )   α
                               ]    α
                           ]ρνω   α
                               ]    α
5                              ]    α
                               ]    α
    ] . [                      ]γος μναῖ δ˙ ἰσχύι α
```

space for 1 line blank

```
    ]κιον γ[                    ] . δινόχρωα
    ]καρίων ε . [               ]ε φορτίω   α
10  ]κια λευκὰ [                ] στρώματα μναῖ η
    ὁ]μοί(ως) στημ[             ] τοῦ στρώμ(ατος) μναῖ δ
    ] . εἰς τὸ λ . [            ]μναιωμ(  ) . . λ(  ) μναῖ α (ἥμισυ)
    ]ς ὀμφαλαδ[                 ] . . . μον   α
    ]ρια    [                   ] γ˙
15  ] . ιτρι[                   ]   α
```

Col. ii

— — — — — — — — — —

```
            δεν[
            πηγ[
            λ . . [
            καδ[
20          σω[
            στ . [
            αμ[
            αμ[
            [
25          [
            [
            α[
            λέβητος [
            ὁμοί(ως) ἄλλο[υ λέβητος
```
                7 ἰσχύει

1 . ονω . (   ): the letter over ω can best be interpreted as π, μ, or λ. A raised μ, however, takes a different form in ll. 11 and 12. As the ο before ν is clear, ἄνω π(όλεως) will not do, even if such a phrase were expected in an account of this nature. There is a slight possibility that the raised letter does not belong to this line but to an insertion above it; if that should be so, then μ(υριάς) or λ(οιπόν) would come into consideration.

7 E.g., στήμω]ρος, but it is not possible to arrange the fragments in such a way that the lines here printed as 11 and 7 could be read together as ὁ]μοί(ως) στήμ[ω]ρος κτλ.

ἰσχύι (l. ἰσχύει) α: 'it is worth' or 'it weighs 1 (mina?)'. This is apparently a remark concerning the 4 minas of yarn (?) just mentioned.

8 Perhaps ῥοδινόχρωα, 'rose-colored', though the term is not found elsewhere. The final α is raised, so the word may be abbreviated.

9]καρίων: the end of a word, or a reference to Carian goods of some kind. For the latter possibility cf. 66.8.

φορτίω: i.e., φορτίῳ or φορτίω(ν). There is no mark of abbreviation, but in this context a genitive would be easier to explain than a dative: if φορτίω(ν) is the word meant, then α will be the price or the weight of the shipments. The preceding ε is reported as certain in the Brussels MS. On the plate]μαφορτίω(ν), 'cloaks', looks worth considering, but it does not seem possible to effect a join between the fragments of the papyrus by reading σο[υβρικο]μαφορτίω(ν).

11 στήμ[ωνος, στημ[ίου, or the like.

12 The word division may be]μναι ωμ(   ); the next word is probably an abbreviation of some form of παλαιός or πάλλιον. Then μναῖ was written, though μνᾶ would be better grammatically.

13 LSJ records 'button' as a meaning of ὀμφαλός. That would suit the context, but it does not seem possible to read a form of ὀμφαλός here.

17 Presumably πηγ[ίου, 'weaver's spool', or πηγ[ίσματος, 'weaver's thread'.

19 The only serious possibilities are κάδ[ου, καδ[ίου, and καδ[μείας.

4. FRAGMENT OF A LETTER

I 5ᶜ + 6ᶜ   (a) 7.5 × 9 cm.   4th cent.
                             (b) 2 × 18.5 cm.

Two non-contiguous fragments of a private letter, too mutilated to yield continuous sense.

```
        τῷ κυρίῳ τῷ α[              ]
        καὶ Εὐναιτ . [
        Κοπρῆς . [
        γίνωσκε . [
   5    ἑτοιμακέναι τα[
        ἀρτάβας τοῦ Τριφ[
        δὲ ἀρτάβην λεγου[          ]μεσι[
        κοντα πέμψογ[             [ . ον δε . [
        αὐτὸ ἀπελυ[                ]μω . [
  10                               ]ελευ[
                                   ]υσια[
                                   ] . σοι[
                                   ] . ε . [
                                   ]σαι . [
  15                               ] . ωσ . [
                                   ]/ ο . [
                                   ] . ονο[
                                   ]δεαι . [
                                   ] . ἐρρῶ[σθαί σε εὔχομαι
  20                      πολλοῖ]ς χρ[ό]νο[ις
```

Back: faint traces of the address.

1   E.g., τῷ ἀ[γαπητῷ ἀδελφῷ.
6   Τριφ[: the only suitable names listed in the *NB* and *Ono-masticon* are Τριφέριος and Τριφιόδωρος. Cf. also **2**.8 with note.

5-15. MISCELLANEOUS FRAGMENTS

In addition to the four texts just printed, the cover of Codex I contains 43 small bits of papyrus dating from the late third to the early fourth century A.D. None of these is extensive enough to permit an identification of the type of document from which it comes, and most contain only slight traces of a few letters. The best preserved are transcribed below.

5. I 7ᶜ + 8ᶜ + 9ᶜ. Three fragments of the same text, measuring respectively 2 × 1, 6 × 2, and 2.5 cm. Text: (a)][[πρὸς αὐτὰ]][(b)] δι' ἐμοῦ Παραμμέους [²]υ ὑπὲρ ὀνομα( )[(i.e., ὀνόμα(τος) or ὀνομά(των). These two fragments apparently preserve an upper margin. (c) contains only traces that are now illegible.

6. I 10ᶜ. 5 × 1.5 cm. Text:] ἰατρὸς καὶ . . . . . [²]στοριατ . [³]θαι[. . .]πατρὸς [. Line 2 could be interpreted as e.g. ἰ]στορία τ . [or ἰ]στορῖ (l. -εῖ) etc.

7. I 11ᶜ + 12ᶜ. Two fragments of one text. (a), 2.5 × 4 cm., is illegible. (b), 1.5 × 3 cm., reads] . . του[²]ονοσ[³] αφ[⁴] . . . . [. There is space sufficient for a line blank between ll. 2 and 3.

8. I 14ᶜ - 17ᶜ. Four fragments of the same text, only one of which offers more than a few traces. Text of (d), 2 × 7 cm.:] . πενο . [²] . παχυ[³]οντα[⁴]μι . υ[⁵] . υ καὶ ε[⁶]επη[. Space enough for two lines is blank between ll. 2 and 3.

9. I 19ᶜ. 2.5 × 1.5 cm. Text:]ων ἡμῶν δ[.

10. I 20ᶜ. 2 × 2 cm. Right margin apparently preserved. Text:] η²]μεν ³] . . . .

11. I 22ᶜ. 4 × 1.5 cm. Text:] προ[.

12. I 25ᶜ. 3 × 2 cm.] . . [²]ντας ὁμοίας βια[³πε]ρὶ παραστ[.

13. I 26ᶜ. 2 × 0.5 cm.]εωμεν[²]μψαμεγ[.

14. I 28ᶜ. 1.5 × 1.5 cm.] . . . [²] . μ . [.

15. I 33ᶜ-4ᶜ. Two bits from the same text. The better preserved (I 33ᶜ, 1.5 × 4.5 cm.) reads]⁻ [²]η [³]γαι [⁴] . απα[⁵] . . . [. The stroke in l. 1 presumably marks a numeral or abbreviation.

CODEX IV

Twenty-six small bits of Greek texts written in hands of the fourth century A.D. So far as the content is identifiable they come from accounts. The large quantities of goods involved suggest that these were official and not private accounts, as is also the case with the documents in the cover of Codex V. The largest and best preserved fragments are transcribed below.

16. IV 1ᶜ. 13.9 × 4.2 cm. Text:] . . . . [²]ον'[. The last letters may be an abbreviation of ὀνόματος.

17. IV 2ᶜ. 6.5 × 3.5 cm. Text:

] . . . . . ρ συνα[.]α . . [	
] . οἴνου σ(πάθια) Γυι''. [	3410 spathia of wine
] Γρμδ', ἀφ' ὧν [	3144, of which

The beginning of l. 1 was read as] . . . υτρ( ) in the Brussels MS, but the ρ appears rather to be a numeral, perhaps preceded by Γ (3000). At the end σὺν ἄ[π]αγτ[ι would suit the traces.

18. IV 3ᶜ. 2.3 × 3 cm. Text:

κρ]ιθῶν (ἀρτ.) [	artabs of barley
]ούτως [	as follows
] . σίτου (ἀρτ.) [	artabs of wheat

19. Two fragments. (*a*) IV 4ᶜ. 1.5 × 2 cm.]ₗ . ω . [²] . . [³] . φμ[. (*b*) IV 5ᶜ. 6.2 × 4.8 cm.] σί(του) . [²traces ³] (ἀρταβῶν?) (μυριάδες) . μς εχ . [⁴] . . κρ(ιθῆς) [. There are ink traces on the back of both fragments, but only an α in the 4th line of the back of (*b*) is clear. The first line of (*a*) is a numeral, the stroke marking a number in the thousands.

20. IV 6ᶜ. 4 × 2.1 cm. Text:] . [²]μων Αἰγύπ[τ]ου δρα[. The word before Αἰγύπ[τ]ου might be νό]μων or νο[μῶν, 'laws, nomes, or meadows of Egypt', but there are other possibilities even if Αἰγύπ[τ]ου does refer to the country; it may, however, be a personal name.

21. IV 21ᶜ. 1.5 × 1 cm. Text: χοι . [(e.g., Χοία[κ). Slight traces of a 2nd line.

CODEX V

22. OFFICIAL ACCOUNTS

The best preserved papyri from the cover of Codex V come from what must have been an extensive series of official accounts in money and kind, dealing with an area at least as large as the Thebaid: their extremely mutilated condition is much to be regretted. The rectos of those fragments which most obviously belong together have been assembled under the number **22**, and such versos of the same fragments as bear decipherable writing under **23**. This assembly has been made very conservatively, very possibly too much so; re-examination of the originals may well show that some pieces here assigned other numbers were in fact once part of the same roll. There appears to be no way of determining the original order of the fragments. The presentation in this edition is arbitrary.

Fragments (c) and (h), as well as **23**(c), were written at a time when the *provincia Thebaidos* was divided into two procuratorships, and presumably all parts of the text are to be dated very closely together. The Thebaid may have become a separate province as early as February A.D. 295; it had certainly done so, and been divided into two ἐπιτροπαί, by September of 298, which is therefore the most cautious terminus post quem for this text. It has been suggested that the two subdivisions had been given up by 323, and if so that year forms a terminus ante, but the evidence is very slight: see P. Beatty Panop. pp. xv-xxi, CPR V 6.7 n.

At least those portions of the accounts preserved in **22**(c) and **23**(c) were concerned with revenues from or for both the Upper and the Lower Thebaid. This suggests that they were drawn up by or intended for use in an office higher than that of the procuratorship of either division. The most obvious instance would be that of the *praeses Thebaidos*.

(a)   V 1ᶜ. 3 × 13 cm. The first few letters from the lines of one column. The back is blank.

$\longrightarrow$ σα[
              κω[
              τ . [
              εισ[

```
        5         υ[
                  π[
                  α . [
                  ạ[
                  . [
       10         α[
                  . [
                  π[
                  κα[
```

— — —

8 ạ may be corrected from another letter.

(b)   V 2ᶜ. 6.2 × 14 cm. The beginning of two lines from the
bottom of a column, with scattered traces of a preceding column.
On the back is **23**(a).

ii

— — —

→   αιϛ[
          κ . [

(c)   V 3ᶜ. 6.6 × 13.8 cm. An account concerning chaff which, if
the seemingly self-evident supplements in lines 3 and 6 are correct,
was collected from or for at least the two divisions of the Thebaid.
The purpose of the chaff is not stated, but the military annona
would be a reasonable guess. Some other documents from about the
time of this text report large requisitions of chaff for the use of
troops temporarily stationed in Egypt because of the unrest of the
last decade of the third century A.D. (P. Oxy. I 43 recto, P. Beatty
Panop.; cf. W. Ensslin in *Aegyptus* 32, 1952, 163-78), but it would
be hazardous to posit a similar background for this papyrus without
further evidence. On the back is **23**(b).

```
→         ἀχύρου
                    οὔ[τως
          ἐπ[ι]τροπῆς Θηβαίδος ἄγ[ω
                 ]υ δι' Ἐπιμάχου ε[
        5              ] διὰ Πλήνιος [
          ἐπιτροπῆς Θ]ηβαί[δος κάτω
                        ] . . . [
                        ] . . . [
```

10

]μαχο[
]υθου[
] . . [

— — —

3 Not ἀπὸ δι]επ[ι]τροπῆς to follow the phrasing of (h).1, as the large epsilon shows that ἐπιτροπῆς was the first word in this line.

4 Probably 'Επιμάχου ἐ[πιμελητοῦ; cf. in general P. Beatty Panop. 1.230-40 n., 276-331 n., P. Oxy. I 43 recto cols. iii-iv.

9 Possibly δι' 'Επι]μάχο[υ as in l. 4, but there are other possibilities, and no good reason to expect the man again here.

(d) V 4ᶜ. 7.1 × 13.5 cm. Fragment of an account in money, collected in large amounts from various localities. (e) comes from a similar account, or may be a further portion of this one. On the back is **23**(c).

— — — — — —

→]	. . [		
] . μις	. [		
]	(ταλ. ?) [		
] . .	(ταλάντων) (μυριάδες) δ[	(40000 [+ ?])
5 πό]λεως	(ταλάντων) (μυριάδες) γ	(30000 tal.)
]	(ταλάντων) (μυριάδες) β ,Ϛ	(26000 tal.)
]πόλε[ω]ς	(ταλάντων) (μυριάδες) β ,Η .	(28000 + tal.)

5 and 7 The possibilities include Ἑρμοῦ πόλεως, Διὸς πόλεως, Λύκων πόλεως, Πανὸς πόλεως, 'Απόλλωνος πόλεως. One expects the city in l. 5 to be different from that in l. 7.

7 This is probably the last line of the column.

(e) V 5ᶜ. 3.5 × 3.5 cm. Fragment of a money account. See (d) introd. The back is blank.

— — — — —

] . [
] (ταλάντων) (μυριάδες) δ [
] ἀπὸ [
]ϛ' [

— — — — —

3-4 ἀπό may have been followed by a place name, and if so that name may have been written wholly or partly in l. 4, i.e., read

instead of the printed text ⁴—πόλεω]ς. But in that case it is odd
that the scribe left so much space after ἀπό, and the trace in l. 4
resembles ε rather than ς, so the pattern may have been ἀπό so
many talents lost in l. 3 followed by another figure in l. 4; that is,
of so many talents due, so many were paid.

(f)   V 6ᶜ. 3 × 4 cm. Fragment of an account in artabs. The back
is blank.

] (ἀρτάβαι) ͵Ϛφ [	(6500 art.)
] (ἀρτάβαι) ͵Γφ [	(3500 art.)

(g)   V 7ᶜ. 9.5 × 10.6 cm. The bottom right side of a column
recording quantities of some substance measured in xestai (e.g., oil
or wine), collected in at least one case by an ἐπιμελητής (8). The
back is blank.

(traces of two lines)

3	]α	
	] ξ(έσται) Δφαd	(4501 1/4 xestai)
5	] ξ(έσται) Γραdη	(3101 3/8 x.)
	] ξ(έσται) Α	(1000 x.)
	] ξ(έσται) Α	(1000 x.)
	] Ἀπολλωνίου ἐπιμελ(ητοῦ) ξ(εστῶν) (μυριὰς) α dη	(10000 3/8 x.)
	] ξ(έσται) χ	(600 x.)

1-7   To judge from the spacing of the writing and the (relatively)
small amounts involved, these lines are parallel to 9 rather than to 8.
It is therefore doubtful whether the names of ἐπιμεληταί should be
expected in lacuna, for in 9 traces of a name should have been
preserved unless it was very much shorter than the name in 8. It
is possible that 8 is a heading which gives the total collected by
the epimeletes named, and that 9 begins a breakdown of that total
according to the assistants through whom it was collected, the
areas from which it was collected, or some other principle. If that
should be the case, lines 1-7 would be the end of a similar breakdown
of a figure now lost.

8 This line no doubt began with διά (cf. e.g. (c).4-5, (h).4ff., (i) etc.), but Apollonius could be either the epimeletes himself or his father.

(h) V 8ᶜ. 10.2 × 16.5 cm. The beginning of an account concerning at least two nomes of the Lower Thebaid; (i) preserves the end of a similar, but not, I think, the same account.* So far as the names of the nomes are preserved, both texts appear to follow the stereotyped order set out in P. Beatty Panop. p. xix: Hermopolite, Antinoite, Kussite, Lycopolite, Hypselite, Apollonopolite, Antaiopolite, Panopolite, Thinite. The Antinoite, however, is not found in its expected position after the Hermopolite in the present fragment, nor does the Thinite follow the Panopolite in (i). Whether they were included at some point in the lost portions of the papyri cannot be determined, but the tables in P. Beatty Panop. p. xix may suggest that omission of some nomes from a given list is more probable than a violation of the standard listing order.

On the back are scattered traces, possibly offsets.

→   ἀπὸ διεπιτροπῆς Θηβαίδος κάτω [

ϛπ . [

Ἑρμοπολίτου   οὕτω[ϛ·

δι(ὰ) Ἰσιδώρο[υ   ] . [

5   δι(ὰ) Αἰλίου [

δι(ὰ) Ἰσιδώ[ρου

οὕτ[ως·

Κουσσ[ίτου

δι(ὰ) Ι[

breaks off

1 The word διεπιτροπή is apparently new. The usual word for the area governed by an ἐπίτροπος of one of the divisions of the Thebaid was ἐπιτροπή: how διεπιτροπή differs from this, if at all, is unclear.

---

* The fragments here published as **22**(h), **24**, **25**, and **22**(i) are illustrated together in the *Facsimile Edition*: *Cartonnage* pl. 13 following an earlier conjecture that they once formed part of the same papyrus sheet, but later study indicates that this will not have been the case. **22**(h) and (i) cannot be convincingly presented as parts of a single list from a roll with a plausible format, and the versos are dissimilar. For the other pieces see **24** introd. and **25**.1-3 n.

(*i*)   V 11^c. 11.1 × 16.5 cm. The end of an account similar to the foregoing; see introd. there, and for the possibility that **25** should be joined to the text see **25** introd. The back contains **23**(*d*).

Col. i

Top lost; the first line preserved is on a level with the tenth line of col. ii.

→]′ δι(ὰ) Θέωνος	(through Theon)
] (μυριάδες?) δ ͵Θ	(49000)
]ι̣σ̣ . . . (ταλάντων) (μυριάδες) β ͵Βσ	(22200 talents)
]ευης (ταλάντων) (μυριάδες) β ͵Ζω	(27800 talents)

Col. ii

5	ʽΥψ]ηλίτου
	] (*traces*)
	] . ρ . . . . . ς
	[ʼΑ]πόλλωνος κά[τω
	[δι(ὰ) ʽΙ]ερακίωνος [
10	δι(ὰ) Ψάιτος Σύρου [
	ʼΑνταιοπολίτ[ου
	δι(ὰ) [
	Πανοπολίτου
	δι(ὰ) ʼΑπολλω( ) ʽΙερακαπ[όλλωνος
15	δι(ὰ) ʼΑπολλωνίδου [
	δι(ὰ) Θεοτίμου καὶ ʽΗρ[
	ἐπὶ τὸ αὐτὸ [

4   The papyrus has been cut away immediately after this line. It may have been the last in the column, as it is on a level with the total in l. 17.

23. FRAGMENTS OF ACCOUNTS

The back of **22** contains fragments of a series of documents written in at least two hands, both different from that of the main text. So far as can be determined, these are accounts, presumably official. Not every piece of **22** has writing on the back, however, and in some which do the verso text is illegible. The following are the best preserved specimens.

(a) V 2ᶜv. 6.2 × 14 cm. Back of **22**(b). Remnants of six lines of unidentified nature.

— — — — —

↓   *traces of two lines*
          ]ευδαι [
          ] . σαεπ[
5   ]αναι [
          ] . . . . ὑπ(ὲρ) [

3 The traces suggest some form of Εὐδαίμων or a similar name.
6 Θη]βαίδ(ος) is just possible.

(b) V 3ᶜv. 6.2 × 13.8 cm. Back of **22**(c). Fragment of an account arranged by nome, with entries in the form "to so-and-so through so-and-so, so much . . ." The first name in such an entry is presumably an official in charge of collecting money or some commodity, and the second an agent of his. What was collected is no longer apparent, but oil may be mentioned in l. 9.

— — — — — —

↓   ] . ε
          ]οπολείτου
          ]αίῳ δι(ὰ) Τιβερίνου π . [.]λι[
                    δι(ὰ) Αγω[
5   ] Ἰουνίῳ δι(ὰ) Μέλανο[ς
          ] δι(ὰ) Σιλβανο[ῦ
          ]ενδεμ[
          Σα]ραπίων[
          ]ελεα κ[
10   ]ετω[
          ]αυ αρ[
          ]ου . [

— — — — — —

1 ἔστι] δέ would seem appropriate.
2 The end of a nome name such as Ἑρμ]οπολείτου. The suitable names from the Lower Thebaid can be found in the list in **22**(h) introd., but that need not be the provenience of this text.
8 Presumably Σα]ραπίων[ι or δι(ὰ) Σα]ραπίων[ος.
9 ἔλεα for ἔλαια, 'oils', seems more reasonable than ἐλέα 'olive tree' or 'olive', but this may be the end of some proper name.

(c) V 4ᶜv. 7.1 × 13.5 cm. Back of **22**(d). Part of two columns of a money account, presumably revenue from some tax, covering the whole of the Thebaid.

Col. i

↓ ⸻ ⸻ ⸻ ⸻ ⸻ ⸻

      ] . .
      ]Βγ
                space for one line blank
   ] ἀπὸ Δι . [.] . . . (τάλαντα) ‚Δ‾   (4000 talents)
   ] . (τάλ.) ‚Αυ   (1400 talents)
5] . (τάλ.) ‚Ζ   (7000 talents)

Col. ii

   ⸻ ⸻ ⸻ ⸻ ⸻

      ]σϲ . [
      ]σαλ[
                traces of two lines
10   ]ειπ . λοι[
      ]δια[
      ]ευδ[
                space for two lines blank
      ὁμοῦ   [
      Θηβ(αίδος) κά[τω
15   Θηβ(αίδος) ἄν[ω
      πα   . [

(ll. 13-5) 'All together . . . for the Lower Thebaid . . . for the Upper Thebaid . . .'

3 Διὸ[ς] πόλ(εως) looks plausible on the plate, but according to the Brussels MS it cannot be read.

11 Presumably διά or δι' Α[.

13 ὁμοῦ was probably followed by a total for the Thebaid as a whole, which the following two lines then break down into revenue from each ἐπιτροπή. The point of l. 16 is altogether unclear.

(d) V 11ᶜv. 11.1 × 16.5 cm. Back of **22**(i). Presumably an account.

↓
— —   —   —   —   —
]ολου ἀπ . [
]   οὗτ(ως)· [
]κτῳ( ) καὶ Σύρου [
] . αχ . . . ( ) οὗτ(ως)· [
5   ]πόλλωνος Κτησίου καὶ 'Αχ[
] Πασήτιος καὶ Λου . . ολ( ) [
] . ατιος 'Απ . . . [.]ω . . [
]πόλλωνος Κορνηλίου πολλὰ ἕτερ(α) . [
] Εὐσεβείων(ος) μ . . . . σιο[

5 and 8 Πόλλωνος, 'Α]πόλλωνος, or a compound such as 'Ιερα-
κα]πόλλωνος.

6 Apparently not Λουκόλ(λου).

24. V 9ᶜ. 4.3 × 4 cm. 4th cent. Fragments of accounts. It has
been suggested that this text is a continuation of **22**(h), and pl. 13
of the *Facsimile Edition: Cartonnage* was composed on that assumption. If so, it comes from a later column than **22**(h), as οὕτω[ς in
l. 3 there cannot have been followed by l. 2 of **24**, with which it
would be level. Too little is preserved to be certain whether the
hand of the front of **24** is the same as in **22**(h) and (i), but that of
the back of **24** is distinctly different from that of **23**(d), the verso
of **22**(i).

Front:

→   ]φγαις'   (551 1/2)
         ]ις
— —   —

Back:

↓   ] . . . . (ταλ.) (μυρ.) . ξ   (more than 10060 talents)
            ] . ''
— —   —

The traces before (ταλ.) in l. 1 of the back text are very faint and
may not be ink.

25. V 10ᶜr. 6.5 × 4 cm. 4th cent. Fragment of a text of uncertain nature. A ship's captain or a related term is mentioned in

l. 1, so shipping is involved in some way. A join with **22**(*i*) is not out of the question; cf. 1-3 n. On the back is **26**.

→   ]   κυβερνητ( )   [
     ] . ια λη( ) Ὠρίων Δημητ[
       ]ερ[. . .] . . . . σω . . . αυ[

1-3   A join of this fragment with **22**(*i*) col. i would give the following result: δι(ὰ) Θέωνος | κυβερνήτ(ου) (ταλ.) (μυρ.) δ ,Θ | . ια λη( ) Ὠρίων Δημήτρις . . . (ταλ.) (μυρ.) β ,Βσ etc., 'through Theon, skipper, 49000 talents . . . Horion (son of?) Demetrius . . . 22200 talents'. Tempting as this appears at first sight, l. 2 of the reconstruction is ungrammatical, and the versos do not favor the join.

1   From κυβερνήτης or a derivative such as κυβερνητικός, case and number uncertain.

2   Presumably λή(μματος) or λη(μμάτων). The preceding word may be διά.

3   Perhaps κυβ]ερ[νήτ]ης Ω . . . αυ[.

26.   V 10ᶜv. 6.5 × 4 cm. 4th cent. Fragment of an account concerning at least one ἐπιμελητής, reporting revenue for a 6th indiction. Written on the back of **25**.

↓   ] . [
   ] . ιανὸς Πε . . τίνου ἐπιμελ(ητοῦ) α[
   ] Σαραπίωνι Διδύμου ἑκτ(ης) ϛ ἰνδ(ικτίων)ο(ς) [
   ] . πίωνος Πάσιος καὶ . . . . ἑκτ(ης) ϛ ἰνδ[(ικτίων)ο(ς)

L. 2 may be translated 'To Sarapion son of Didymos, for the sixth (6th) indiction . . .'

27.   V 12ᶜ. 2.8 × 4.9 cm. 4th cent. Fragment of an official account concerning ἐπιμεληταί. The text is on the back of the document, the fibers on the front having been stripped off.

↓   ] . [   ]‾
     Σ]εουήρο(υ) ἐπιμελ(ητοῦ) [
     ]υπορος ἐπιμε[λ(ητοῦ)

```
      ] . ωδος π . . ρο(  )   [
5     Διδ]ύμου ἐπιμελ(ητοῦ) [
      ]υ ἐπιμ[ελ(ητοῦ)
```

1   The high stroke marks a numeral or abbreviation.

3   The remnants of the name suggest Ε]ὔπορος, though one rather expects a genitive.

28. V 13ᶜr. 5 × 14 cm. 4th cent. Fragment of an account, or possibly of a contract. On the back is **29**.

```
→        το]ῦ παρελθόγ[τος
         ]ε . . ποι . [
          ] . . π . . . . [
           ] . ασαυ .            [
5        ]συναγαν(  ) (τάλ.) . μη κ[
         ] (τάλ. ?) ξ̣           [
         ] . . ως π . . [
         ] . σιλο . ωϲα [
               traces of 1 line
```

1   το]ῦ παρελθόγ[τος ἔτους or μηνός.
5   Not συναγόμ(ενα).

29. V 13ᶜv. 5 × 14 cm. Fragment of an account, probably official. On the front is **28**.

Traces of two lines of a column to the left, then:

col. ii

```
↓                    δ[ι(ὰ) . [
                     δι(ὰ) Ὠρ[
        λή(μματα) . . . [
                     δι(ὰ) . [
5                    δι(ὰ) [
                     δι(ὰ) Ὠ[
        λή(μματα) Φε . . [
                     δι(ὰ) ⟦Τιμο⟧ Θεο̣[
                     δι(ὰ) Ἀχιλλέω[ς
```

10   δι(ὰ) Διοσκόρου [
            δι(ὰ) Δ[
            δ[ι(ὰ)

—   —   —   —   —

3, 7   The word after λή(μματα) may be the name of the place in which the following collectors were active or the name of the supervisor for whom they worked.

30.   V 14ᶜ. 4.2 × 3.6 cm. 4th cent. Fragment of an account. The back is blank.

—   —   —   —   —

→   *traces of* 1 *line*
     ]ατενοῦτος δι(ὰ) . [
    ᾽Ι]σχυρίωνος δι(ὰ) [
     ]μωνος   [

—   —   —   —   —

4   E.g., Χαιρή]μωνος, Εὐδαί]μωνος.

31.   V 15ᶜ. 4.2 × 3.5 cm. 3rd-4th cent. Copy of a document of uncertain nature. The back is blank.

—   —   —   —

→   ἀντίγραφον [
    Κλαύδιος Α[
    περὶ Χην[οβόσκια

—   —   —   —

3   περὶ Χην[οβόσκια: cf. **1**.4 n. περὶ χην[ῶν, χην[οβοσκῶν, 'about geese, gooseherds' or the like is improbable, as it is most natural to take this line as part of the man's origo or the place where he served some public function.

32-43

In addition to the pieces printed as **22-31**, the cover of Codex V contained forty-seven tiny fragments which bear writing, for the most part too small and damaged for transcription. Some may belong together, or to texts published above, but this can hardly be determined in their present condition. The larger are transcribed below. Unless the contrary is noted, the backs are blank. All probably belong to the early fourth century A.D.

32.   V 16ᶜ. 5 × 5 cm.

     — — — — — —
     ]λοϲιϲπῳ . [
     ] . γοϲαπο[.] . . . [
     ]ον Πανίϲκου [
       ] . α . . . α . [
     — — — — — —

33.   V 17ᶜ. 3 × 2.6 cm.

     — — — — — —
     ] διὰ ᾿Απολ . [
       ]λαυ[
     — — — — — —

34.   V 18ᶜ. 2 × 3.9 cm.

     — — — —
     ]ου . αι[
     ]ανεγ[
     — — — —

35.   V 19ᶜ. 2 × 2.8 cm.

     — — — —
     ] . [
     ] θ . [
     — — — —

36.   V 20ᶜ. 2.3 × 2.8 cm.

     — — — — — —
     ] (ἀρταβῶν) (μυρ.) α . [
     — — — — — —

37.   V 21ᶜ. 3 × 3 cm.

     — — — — —
     ] . . . ωϲ . . . [
       ] διὰ Φ[
     — — — — —

     Back: *traces of 1 line*

38.   V 22ᶜ. 1.2 × 4.5 cm.

     — — — —
     ] . [
     ]ωρ( )[
     — — — —

   Back

     — — — —
     ] (ταλ.) [
     ] . . [
     — — — —

39. V 23ᶜ. 1.2 × 2.7 cm. — — — —
]ατν[
] . . δι[
— — — —

40. V 24ᶜ. 2.1 × 1 cm. — — —
]ον [
— — —

41. V 25ᶜ. 2 × 1.8 cm. — — — —
]ἒπαρχι . [
— — — —

42. V 26ᶜ. 2 × 1.1 cm. — — — —
]α . . . [

Back — — — —

— — — — —
] δι(ὰ) Θεο[
— — — — —

43. V 35ᶜ. 2.8 × 1.8 cm. — — — — — — —
]ε[
ʽΗρ]αxλέου δι(ὰ) [
— — — — — —

CODEX VI

44. Five fragments of a name list, evidently intended for taxation purposes. About 1.5 cm. was originally left free between each name. In some instances a further name, usually somewhat indented, was later written in this free space: these entries are more cursive than the original text, but may nevertheless have been made by the same scribe. Three entries in frag. (*a*) bear a marginal note, ζ(ήτησον), 'find him' or 'investigate'. In one case this note was then cancelled.

Although as much as 3.5 cm. of blank papyrus is found to the right of some names, no statement of money or goods owed is preserved, so the nature of the charge concerned remains obscure. Almost all the persons listed were men, but a woman probably appears in (*b*).5. The original order of the fragments can no longer be determined; that used in this edition is arbitrary. Late 3rd or early 4th century A.D. On the back is **45**.

The Brussels MS included no transcripts of texts from the cover of Codex VI. The readings of **44-61** are therefore based exclusively on photographs and must be accepted with appropriate caution.

(*a*) VI 1ᶜ recto. 10 × 14.5 cm.

$$\longrightarrow$$

— — — —

traces

Φατρῆς ἀδελφός

ζ(ήτησον) Παγαμεὺς Σεναμούνιος

Παχυρᾶς Σέρβιος

5 Διόσκορος Φαήριος Δελχοῦ απα[

⟦ζ(ήτησον)⟧ Φαῆρις Πενδ . εῦτος

ζ(ήτησον) Φαῆρις Μίδου

[Διό]σκορος Ἡρακλήους

Τούρβων Φαήριος

10 Ἧλις Πλοῦτος νε[

ˌΦαῆρις Π[

Κυ[

— — — —

2 and 4: later additions.

4 Παχυρᾶς Σέρβιος: both names are new if rightly read, but there

is considerable doubt about the first, which is very cursively written;
cf. however Κῦρος and Κῦρα. Σέρβιος, though genitive, may have
been derived from Latin Servius.

5   Δελχοῦ is not in *NB* or *Onomasticon*. Cf. Δολχοῦς.

ᾳπα[: e.g., ἀπα[ιτητής, ἄπα NN, ἀπ' Α[.

6   Πενδ . εὗτος: new. The name Διεύς is well known, but Πενδιεῦ-
τος is not probable, as the descender of an iota should be visible.
Possible no letter has been lost, though in that case the delta was
written unusually large.

10   νε[ωτέρου is an obvious supplement, but a name such as
Νε[οπτολέμου or a trade beginning with νε- is also possible.

11   The significance of the mark before Φαῆρις is not clear.

(*b*)   VI 2ᶜ recto. 9.5 × 14 cm.

```
    —  —    —    —    —    —
→                    ]ς
                  ]αχανᾶς
              Διο]σκόρου ταπη
              ] . υς ἀδελφός
5             ] . αμινία Χαλέου 'Ελέως
              Διόσκορος ἀδελφός
              Σανσνῶς Χολλῶτος
              ] . . [ . ] . [ . . ]ς ἀδελφός
              ]ω[ . ] ἄλλος ἀδελφός
10            ἀ]δελφ(ός)
                  ] . [
    —    —    —    —    —
```

7 and 10:   later additions.

2   Probably λ]αχανᾶς, 'vegetable gardener'.

3   If ταπη(τάριος) is meant there is no sign of abbreviation.
Possibly therefore the genitive of Ταπῆς: that name is not in *NB* or
Onomasticon, but cf. Ταφῆς and Ταπῆσις.

4   The first name is probably Φαμινία.

(*c*)   VI 3ᶜ recto. 2 × 5.5 cm.

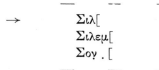

```
    —    — —    —
→         Σιλ[
          Σιλεμ[
          Σογ . [
    —    —    —
```

2 No name beginning with Σιλεμ- is recorded in *NB* or *Ono-masticon*.

(*d*) VI 5ᶜ recto. 2.5 × 14 cm.

→ Φαῆρις πρε[
    Παναμεὺς [
    Πάρσυρος
    [
5   Φαῆρις νε[
    Φαῆρις Κελ[
    Πανισνεὺς [
    [Σ]ανσνῶς Μ[

1 A comparison with l. 5 suggests πρε[σβύτερος here and νε[ώτερος there, but of course there are other possibilities.
3 Πάρσυρος: not in *NB* or *Onomasticon*.
4 Stripped away.
5 Cf. 1 n.

(*e*) VI 6ᶜ recto. 7.5 × 9.5 cm.

→]ων Τριαδέλφου
    ]ων Πεκύσιος Σικλῆτος
    ]αβῦγχις Κέντις
    ]ρος Καρούριος

2 Σικλῆτος: not in *NB* or *Onomasticon*.
3 Κέντις = Κέντιος.
4 This appears to have been the last line of the column.

45. The reverse side of **44**, probably written in the same hand as that text, apparently contains lists of two types. The first, represented by fragment (*a*), follows the format of **44** and may be a continuation of it, though cf. n. to l. 4. The lines on the remaining fragments are written much closer together than in **44** and **45**(*a*), and in at least three instances the names were followed by some commodity: wine in (*b*).11, something measured in myriads in (*b*).13 and 14. The impression remains that taxation of some sort is concerned, but that it is different from that of the front text and fragment (*a*).

The text on this side of the papyrus is considerably more worn, discolored, and difficult to decipher than **44**. The fragments are ordered following the presentation of **44**, as there is no clue as to their actual relative positions.

(*a*)　VI 1ᶜ verso. 10 × 14.5.

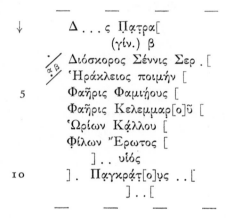

3　Σέννις = Σέννιος. The name appears to be new. The marginal note seems to be of the same sort as that in l. 4; cf. note there.

4　The marginalia, if such they are, here and in l. 3, are quite unintelligible to me. There is some possibility that they are in fact line ends from a preceding column, i.e., that the reading should be (μυριὰς)]α/Β, '12000'. If so, then despite the greater spacing between the lines the content of this account probably resembled that of (*b*) more closely than that of the recto text **44**.

5　Φαμιήους: apparently not Φαμιγοῦς. Neither name is known, but the latter would have had obvious kindred to Φαμῖνις, Φαμίνιος and the like.

6　Κελεμμαρ[ο]ῦ: even if the dotted letters are wrong the name is new.

9　Added between the lines.

(*b*)   VI 2ᶜ verso. 9.5 × 14 cm.

— — — — —

↓　　　. . [
　　　Πλελο[ῦ]ς (?) [
　　　traces
　　　Ἐπώνυχος [
5　　　Κεραπουβεὺς Αλ[
　　　Παῦλος Π . . αιϛ[
　　　Φαῆρις ἀδελφός [
　　　Μακάριος ἄλλος ἀδελφ[ός
　　　Σιλβανὸς Καλει . . δ[.] . [
10　　Διόσκορος Ἀλέως . . . . . [
　　　Φίλων ἀδελφὸς οἴνου [
　　　　　Ἄρριος υἱός
　　　Παγαμεὺς Νεμεσιαγοῦ (μυρ.) [
　　　Μα . . ῷς Ὀπειώνιος (μυρ.) [
15　　Διόσκορος ἀδελφός [
　　　Ὀνγῶφρις Η . ου[
　　　Ζήνων Διοσκο[

— — — — —

2 and 4   There is some discoloration before the first letter read in each of these lines, possibly marginalia or stray ink, possibly also not ink.

5   The division between the names is not quite certain, but the text is probable. Κεραπουβεύς is in that case new.

9   The mutilated name after Σιλβανός appears to be new.

11   Added between the lines.

14   Both names are apparently new.

17   Διοσκό[ρου, Διοσκο[ῦτος, Διοσκο[υρίδου or the like.

The remaining versos of **44** are too mutilated for transcription. I make out only two full words with reasonable certainty, Παῶς ἀδελ(φός) in the 4th line of frag. (*d*) (VI 5ᶜ verso).

46.   VI 4ᶜ recto. 3 × 5 cm. 3rd-4th cent. Remnants of two columns mentioning barley. In the *Facsimile Edition: Cartonnage* p. 19 this papyrus is placed among the fragments of **44** because the hands of the two texts are similar. They do not, however, have the same format, and the hands of the versos (**47** and **45**) differ distinctly from each other.

Col. i				Col. ii
— — — —				— — — —
] *traces*				Η[
			5	Σ . [
]⌐				Κε[
] κρι(θῆς) (ἀρτάβης) ϛ				Ο . [
— — — —				Κ̣ερα[
				’Αχ[
				— — — —

The traces of l. 1 cover all or nearly all of the intercolumnar space of 1.5 cm. It is probably the end of an exceptionally long line of col. i, but it could also be a heading covering both columns. Line 3 translates '1/2 artab of barley'. Between ll. 1 and 2 space enough for one line contains no writing.

47. VI 4ᶜ verso. 3 × 5 cm. 3rd-4th cent. A name list, written on the back of **46**.

↓   Παισᾶς . . [
            Ψαρφει . [
            Σενθα[
            Πενθ . [
5   ϛ . . . υπ[
            ϛΣενφ . [
            ϛΠ[. .]κ̣[

1   Probably the top of the document, or at least of this list.

48. VI 7ᶜ. 5 × 13.5 cm. 3rd-4th cent. About 1.5 cm. from the top of the recto is the note (ἀρούρης) ϛη[, '(at least) 5/8 of an aroura'. The remainder of this side is blank.

Back:

↓   ]ϛ Σοκῆτος β . [
                      3.5 cm. blank
       ] . ῀Ωρος Φιλουμ[ένου
       ]βd
                 traces of at least 1 line
5   ]ϛ Καλῆτο̣[ϛ

1   The name Σοκῆϛ is not in *NB* or *Onomasticon*. Cf. Σοκεύς.

49. VI 8ᵉ. 3.5 × 12 cm. 3rd-4th cent. The recto is blank. The verso contains a name list.

—   —   —

↓   Γεώρ[γ]ι̣[ο]ς̣ [
        Εμποσ[
        Μῶρος Φ[
        Ἐπώνυχ̣[ος

4 cm. blank, then a few letters from four more lines.

2 Εμποσ may be the full name or only its beginning. In either case it appears to be new.

50. VI 9ᶜ recto. 3.5 × 14.5 cm. Grain account, 3rd-4th cent. A further strip of papyrus, VI 10 (0.5 × 7.5 cm.) may belong to the same document. On the back is **51**.

→   ] . μμάχη
        ] Τε̣ῶ̣ς (ἀρτ.) β
        ] (ἀρτ.) εϛ″ κρ(ιθῆς) (ἀρτ.) ϛ″
        ] . ηβης γ″ Ἀβὼ (ἀρτ.) α[
5   ]„
        ] . . ταρα (ἀρτ.) α
        ] κρ(ιθῆς) (ἀρτ.) α̅ς̅γ̅ιβ
        ] (ἀρτ.) α
        ] . . . . . [
10   ] κρ(ιθῆς) (ἀρτ.) ϛ″
        ] .
        ] (ἀρτ.) d
        ] .
        ] .
15   ] . (ἀρτ.) α
        ] (ἀρτ.) . κρ(ιθῆς) (ἀρτ.) . [

51. VI 9ᶜ verso. 3.5 × 14.5 cm. A grain account, written on the back of **50** in a clumsier hand and with a thicker pen than that text. The document may record grain dues collected from the persons listed. 3rd-4th cent.

↓ κλ( ) Ἐπω[
   ᴸʼ Π . α . . ρ[
   κλ( ) Φαησ[
   Λολ'οῦ Πι[
5 ᴸʼ Φαῆρ(ις) . [
   Μέρσις Π[
    (ἀρτ.) δς
   ᴸʼ κρι(θῆς) (ἀρτ.) Ld
   Ἀτρῆ Ἐπ[
10 ᴸ Ἀτρῆς
   Μέρσις Πε[
   ᴸ . . . . . [

1 κλ( ): in all likelihood κλ(ηρονόμοι), with the following name in the genitive, but the possibility of Κλ(αύδιος) NN cannot be entirely disregarded. So also in l. 3.

2 The meaning of the symbol before the name is not clear to me. In l. 8 a similar symbol means (ὧν).

52. VI 11ᶜ. 3 × 6 cm. Name list, 3rd-4th cent. Possibly complete at top and bottom. The text below stands on the recto; the verso contains two notes, καὶ (πυροῦ) ας 'and 1½ (artabs) of wheat' and then after two cm. blank space πας''', '81½', plus a trace of a third line.

→ Πεκῦσις Μ[
   ᴸʼ Μαθεία[ς
   Σεγφαῆρις [
   Σενεβοῦνις [
1 Ψεντεκῶσις . [
   . . οιβελῶς [
    2.5 cm. blank

2 For the sign before the name cf. **51**.2 n.

4 and 5 Neither name is in *NB* or *Onomasticon*. The formation of the second from Τεκῶσις is fully regular.

53. VI 12ᶜ + 13ᶜ. Two disconnected fragments of a document apparently addressed to a strategus or epistrategus, presumably therefore a petition, report, or official correspondence. 3rd-4th cent. The back of both fragments is stained but bears no writing.

(*a*)   VI 12ᶜ. 3 × 10 cm.

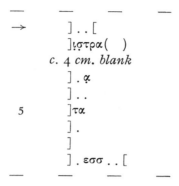

```
→        ] . . [
         ]ιϲτρα(  )
      c. 4 cm. blank
         ] . α̣
         ] . .
5        ]τα
         ] .
         ]
         ] . εϲϲ . . [
```

Col. ii. The writing begins at the level of col. i l. 3.

```
         ὑπ[
10       δε[
         τα[
         δε[
```

(*b*)   VI 13ᶜ. 3 × 4 cm.

```
         ] . [ . ] . [
         ]θιϲ
15       ]ην
         ]η
         ] .
```

2   Presumably the dative of a third-declension name followed by ϲτρα(τηγῷ) or ϲτρα(τηγήϲαντι), or NN ἐπ]ιϲτρα(τήγῳ) or ἐπ]ι-ϲτρα(τηγήϲαντι).

54.   VI 14ᶜ. 3 × 10 cm. 3rd-4th cent. The first few letters of ten lines of a name list, written against the fibers. The other side is blank.

—   —   —   —

↓   *traces of two lines*
      'Επ . . ε[
      Ε . . βαι[
5   Πικῶ[ς
      'Αβῶς [
      Ψενε . [
      Καιυ . ερ[
      Ψενε[
10   Φαῆρις [
      c. 4 cm. blank

3   Of the names in *NB* and *Onomasticon*, 'Επέγε[τος for 'Επαίνετος appears the most attractive.

4   The letter after Ε is probably π or τ. The name is apparently new.

8   I cannot reconcile the traces with any name beginning with Κα- in *NB* or *Onomasticon*. Perhaps simply καὶ ὑπέρ should be read.

55.   VI 15ᶜ. 6.5 × 7 cm. Account, 3rd-4th cent. The back is blank.

—   —   —   —

→   ] . . [
      ] . μίαν . [
      ] . ἡμίσους . [
      ] Θὼθ μόνος με[τ]ρ[
5   ]γίας
      ]′ ια′
      ]„

—   —   —   —

Col. ii. Traces of two lines, beginning at the level of col. i l. 6.

5   μόνος: not μόνον. The last word in the line is a form of μέτρον, μετρέω, or a related term.

6-7   The strokes mark numerals or abbreviations.

56.   VI 16ᶜ. 3.5 × 7 cm. The front bears only a large δ accompanied by a numeral stroke. The back contains the remnants of a text of uncertain nature. 3rd-4th cent.

↓   *traces of 2 lines*
         ]περ . . . . [
         c. 5 cm. blank
         ]στρα( ) . . [

4 Presumably some form of στρα(τηγός), ἐπι]στρά(τηγος), or the related verbs. The traces at the end of the line are unclear and may not be ink.

57. VI 17ᶜ. 7 × 7.5 cm. 3rd-4th cent. On the front only the letters ιβιωνος are preserved: this might be interpreted as the word ἰβιῶνος, 'of the Isis shrine' (at this date probably a place name) or as the personal name ᾽Ιβίωνος, 'of Ibion'. There is a lacuna before ιβιωνος in which another word may have stood, but the spacing forbids a reading such as Φ]ιβίωνος.

Back: account of uncertain nature. The text is:

             traces of 1 line
↓   ]ς
       ]εως Μάρτης
       ]ψειθ β′ τεκ( ) θρι( )
            space for 1 line blank
5   ] .
       ]εράπις
       ] . χ( ) ψαρ . . ε( ) σπου( ) τω
       ]η
       ] . ε ιβ′
10   ] . [

4 τεκ(των), Τεκ(ῶσις), or the like if the reading is correct.
6 Σ]εράπις or a compound.

58. VI 18ᶜ recto. 3.5 × 4.5 cm. Grain account, 3rd-4th cent. On the back is **59**.

→   β]ουκόλου Στο . [
         ] .
         ]ως ⟦(ἀρτ.) . ⟧ ʽ(ἀρτ.) η′ [(8 art.)

```
    ] . (ἀρτ.) ϛ'[                    (½ art.)
5   ]ας (ἀρτ.) αγ[                    (1⅓ art.)
          ] . [
```
—   —   —   —

1 β]ουκόλου, 'herdsman', or the name Βουκόλος. This is probably the first line of the column.

59. VI 18ᶜ verso. 3.5 × 4.5 cm. Text of uncertain nature, 3rd-4th cent. On the front is **58.**

```
↓        ]βαι μδϛ' δ        (44½, 4)
         space for 1 line blank
         ] . σκη            (228)
         ] ἡμῖν             (for us)
         ἀρ]γυριο-          (silver-)
```
—   —   —   —

4 Unless one assumes a false line division, this seems to be a compound word with ἀργύριον as one of its elements, although all similar words in *LSJ*, *WB*, and *Spoglio Lessicale* are built on ἄργυρος.

60. VI 19ᶜ. 4 × 5.5 cm. 3rd-4th cent. The front contains discolorations which may be offsets if they are ink. On the back, traces of six or seven lines, in the first of which the word καί may be recognized.

61. VI 25ᶜ. 3.7 × 2.6 cm. 3rd-4th cent. Fragment of a name list. The text is written against the fibers, the other side being blank.

—   —   —   —
```
↓        ]θ' Πασσῆβις [
         ] Πασσῆβθις [
         ] Φαῆρις Σι . . [
         ] καὶ Πασ[
```
—   —   —   —

1-2 Neither name is recorded in this form in *NB* or *Onomasticon*. For the first cf. Πασῆβις, for the second Πατσέβθις with its numerous variants.

3 The second name is probably Σιρίω[νος or Σίφω[νος.

In addition to the papyri just described, Codex VI contained twenty-one minor bits measuring on the average less than a square centimeter. Several are virtually blank, none yield more than a few generally doubtful letters.

CODEX VII

62. DEED OF SALE

VII 1^c   4.2 × 15 cm.   late 3rd-4th cent.

Virtually all details of the sale recorded on this fragment have been lost, but lines 4-5 present a puzzle of some interest. To judge from the structure of such documents as P. Cair. Isid. 92 and 104, either a regnal year or a consular date is expected in this position. Among the imperial and consular names that occurred during the period in which the papyrus can be placed on palaeographic grounds, the traces preserved would suit a Greek transliteration of Domitius, Vettius, or Tettius. Men of these names served as consuls in A.D. 316, 328, 333, 336, and 372, but I find no convincing way of restoring a known dating formula by the consuls of any of these years in the text.[1] The probability, then, is that the date was given as a regnal year: the only serious possibilities appear to be Aurelian and the rebel Domitius Domitianus. Palaeography and the comparatively late date of the other documents used in this cover favor the latter (probably A.D. 297-8); but interesting as it would be to have a second attestation of Domitianus' revolt from Upper Egypt,[2] the arguments for placing this text in his reign are by no means conclusive.[3]

For the chronology of Aurelian, see P. Oxy. XL pp. 15ff.; for

---

[1] Theoretically Flavius Domitius Leontius, consul in A.D. 344, should also be considered, but the papyri dated by his consulship which have been published up to now omit the name Domitius; references in R. S. Bagnall and K. A. Worp, *The Chronological Systems of Byzantine Egypt* (Zutphen, 1978) p. 111.

[2] It may be assumed that **62** comes from Upper Egypt, as all known places that are referred to in the papyri from these covers were located there. The rebellion is attested at Coptus in P. Mich. III 220.

[3] The discussion above presupposes that the reading of l. 5 in the Brussels MS (in agreement with *Prel. Rep.* p. 12),].ετίου, is correct, and from a photograph that interpretation of the traces appears unobjectionable; but a restoration along the following lines also looks plausible: [ὡμολ(όγησα). ὑπατείας Φλαουίων Λεο]ντίου ⁶[καὶ Σαλλουστίου τῶν λαμπροτά]των. In that case the date would be A.D. 344, which would fall within the time span of the other dated texts from Codex VII (A.D. 341-8, **63-65**).

that of Domitianus, J. D. Thomas, *ZPE* 22 (1976) 253-79 and
24 (1977) 233-40, with the literature cited in those articles. The
papyrus has been mentioned in *Prel. Rep.* p. 12, where the date was
tentatively given as 333 or 336. The back is blank.

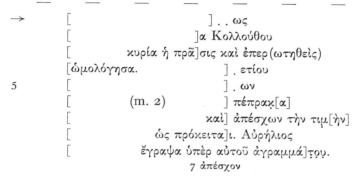

→   [   ] . . ως
       [   ]α Κολλούθου
       [κυρία ἡ πρᾶ]σις καὶ ἐπερ(ωτηθεὶς)
       [ὡμολόγησα.   ] . ετίου
5   [   ] . ων
       [(m. 2)   ] πέπραχ[α]
       [καὶ] ἀπέσχων τὴν τιμ[ὴν]
       [ὡς πρόκειτα]ι. Αὐρήλιος
       [ἔγραψα ὑπὲρ αὐτοῦ ἀγραμμά]τ̲ο̲υ̲.
                        7 ἀπέσχον

(l. 3) 'The sale is valid, and in response to the formal question I
have so declared. (Date). I, NN, have sold . . . and received the
price . . . as stated. I, Aurelius NN, wrote on his behalf, as he is
illiterate.'

4   ὡμολόγησα perhaps abbreviated. For the following date see
introd.
5   E.g., Πα]χών, or λαμπροτά]των if the suggestion on p. 52 n. 3.
is correct.
8   At the start of the line, probably ἐκ πλήρους or a similar
expression.

63. LOAN OF WHEAT

VII 2ᶜ   8.5 × 17 cm.   20 November A.D. 341

A loan of what must have been 1⅔ artabs of wheat, since the
amount to be repaid with the usual increase of fifty percent came
to 2½ artabs. The papyrus evidently comes from a poorly-docu-
mented area of Egypt—the vicinity of Diospolis Parva would be
a reasonable guess—and does not follow the phraseology current in
better known districts of the country. In the lack of a good parallel
I have therefore largely refrained from restorations in the first eight
damaged lines. The general sense of the text, however, is doubtful
only in the penalty clause ll. 5-6. For the reader's convenience I

have accordingly given a hypothetical reconstruction in the first note below.

For juristic discussion of loans in papyri see H. Kühnert, *Zum Kreditgeschäft in den hellenistischen Papyri Ägyptens bis Diokletian* (Freiburg, 1966) and H. A. Rupprecht, *Untersuchungen zum Darlehen im Recht der graeco-aegyptischen Papyri der Ptolemäerzeit* (*Münchener Beiträge* 51, 1967).

—— —— —— —— —— —— ——

```
→       σοι μέτρ[ῳ                                      ]
        μετὰ καὶ [                          ἡμιο-]
        λείας ἄνευ [πάσης ἀντιλογίας καὶ ὑπερθέ-]
        σεως. εἰ δὲ [μὴ ἀποδῶ      ἐξέστω]
5       σοι χρήσα[σθαι                        ]
        εὐπορείᾳ [μέχρι ἀποδόσεως τοῦ εἰρη-]
        μένου σίτου . [                      ]
        καὶ βέβαιον [              ὁ ἐφ᾽ ὑπο-]
        γραφῆς τ[οῦ ὑπὲ]ρ ἐμ[οῦ ὑ]πογρά-
10      φοντος ἐξεδόμην σοι πρὸς ἀσφάλ(ειαν)
        καὶ ἐπερωτηθ(εὶς) ὡμολόγησα.
        ὑπατείας ᾿Αντωνίου Μαρκελλίνου καὶ
        Πετρωνίου Προβίνου τῶν λαμπροτάτω(ν),
        ῾Αθὺρ κδ᾽᾽. (2nd hd.) Αὐρήλιος Ψενετῦ-
15      μις ὁ προκ(είμενος) ἔσχον τὰς τοῦ πυροῦ
        ἀρτάβας δύο ἥμισυ καὶ [ἀ]ποδώσω
        ὡς πρόκ(ειται). Αὐρ(ήλιος) Στατίλλιος Δευ-
        τέρου ἄρξ(ας) τῆς π(όλεως) ἔγραψα ὑπ(ὲρ αὐτοῦ) γράμ-
        ματα μὴ εἰδότος
Back:
20→    χιρώγραφω<ν> Ψενετῦμις
```

18 ὑπ(ὲρ αὐτοῦ): Pap. υ)   20 χειρόγραφον Ψενετύμιος.

'(I, Aurelius Psenetymis, acknowledge receipt from you, NN, of a loan of 2½ artabs of wheat including interest at fifty percent; and this I shall return) to you by (such-and-such) a measure (together with the interest at fifty percent) with no dispute or delay. If I do not make the return ... you may use ... property until the return of the aforementioned grain. (This contract), which I have for your security given to you with the subscription of my signatory, (is valid) and firm, and when asked the formal question I so declared.

Consulship of Antonius Marcellinus and Petronius Probinus, *viri clarissimi*, Hathyr 24. (m. 2) I, the aforementioned Aurelius Psenetymis, have received the two and a half artabs of wheat and I shall return them as stated. I, Aurelius Statillius, son of Deuteros, former magistrate of the city, wrote on his behalf, as he is illiterate. (back) Cheirograph of Psenetymis.'

1-8   A plausible reconstruction might run as follows:

ἃς καὶ ἀποδώσω]

1   σοι μέτρ[ῳ δεκάτῳ ἕως Μεσορὴ λ]
    μετὰ καὶ [τῆς ἀνειλημμένης ἡμιο-]
    λείας ἄνευ [πάσης ἀντιλογίας καὶ ὑπερθέ-]
    σεως. εἰ δὲ [μὴ ἀποδῶ τῇ προθεσμίᾳ, ἐξέστω]
5   σοι χρῆσα[σθαι τῇ παντοίᾳ μου πάσῃ]
    εὐπορείᾳ [μέχρι ἀποδόσεως τοῦ εἰρη-]
    μένου σίτου. κ[ύριον τὸ γράμμα τοῦτο]
    καὶ βέβαιον [ἁπλοῦν γραφέν, ὃ ἐφ' ὑπο-]
    γραφῆς κτλ.

2-3   ἡμιο]λείας: see N. Lewis, *TAPA* 76 (1945) 126-39. The reconstruction proposed above is based on P. Amh. II 147.7, σὺν καὶ τῇ ἀνιλημμένῃ ἡμιολείᾳ. Μετά occasionally replaces σύν elsewhere, e.g. in P. Mich. XI 614.21.

3   Possibly εὑρησιλογίας as in P. Mich. 614.19-20 instead of ἀντιλογίας, but **64.**14 has ἀντιλογίας. Not κρί]σεως, as the examples of ἄνευ κρίσεως καὶ πάσης ἀντιλογίας cited in the *WB* are all Ptolemaic (s.v. ἀντιλογία). The commonest phrase to express the idea is ἀνυπερθέτως καὶ ἄνευ πάσης ἀντιλογίας.

4   After ἀποδῶ supply τῇ προθεσμίᾳ (SB VI 9189.21 with Wilcken's correction recorded there), καθὰ γέγραμμαι (P. Mich. 614.20), ὡς πρόκειται, or the like.

5-6   I know no parallel for the phrase expressed in these lines. If the reconstruction proposed above is along the right lines, the creditor had full use of the debtor's property in case of default, but it is not altogether certain that the infinitive χρῆσα[σθαι rather than the participle should be restored, nor that εὐπορεία is governed by it. That a loan should be secured by all a debtor's property, however, is in itself commonplace.

17   Δευτέρου: not δεύτερος, though that may have been intended, as the name is not recorded in *NB* or *Onomasticon*. **64.**4-5 indicates

that a patronymic is expected, however, and Pape records Δευτέρα
and Δευτέριος. Cf. also Latin Secundus.

18 ἄρξ(ας) τῆς πόλ(εως): cf. Oertel, *Liturgie* 313-16.

64. LOAN OF WHEAT

VII 3ᶜ   9 × 13.1 cm.   21 November A.D. 346

A loan of 3⅚ artabs of wheat, with no mention of interest.
Written against the fibers. The other side is blank.

```
↓        ὑπατείας τῶν δεσποτῶν ἡμῶν
         Κωνσταντίου Αὐγούστου τὸ δ'' καὶ
         Κώνσταντος Αὐγούστου τὸ γ'', Ἀθὺρ κε''.
         Αὐρ(ήλιος) Κόμης Ἁρμογῖτος ἀπὸ κώμης Τεχθὺ
5        τοῦ Διοσπολίτου νομοῦ Αὐρ(ηλίῳ) Πτολεμαίῳ
         Παχούμιος ἄρξ(αντι) τῆς Τεντυριτῶν
         πόλεως χαίρειν. ὁμολογῶ ἐσχη-
         κέναι παρὰ σοῦ καὶ ἠριθμῆσθαι χρῆς[ιν]
         σίτου ἀρταβῶν τριῶν ἡ[μίσου]ς τρίτου,
10       '(γίνονται) (ἀρτάβαι) γLγ', ἃς' καὶ ἀποδώσω σοι καιρ[ῷ τῆς
                                              συγκ]ομ[ι-]
         δῆς τῆς εὐτυχῶς ἐσομ[ένης κατασπορᾶς]
         τῆς ς'' ἰνδικτίωνος ἀ[νυπερθέτως ἐν]
         κόκκῳ τῷ μέτρῳ Φα . [        ἄνευ]
         πάσης ἀντιλογίας, τῆς π[ράξεως]
15       οὔσης ἔκ τε ἐμοῦ καὶ ἐκ [τῶν]
         ὑπαρχόν[των] μου [πάντων μέχρι ἀπο-]
         δόσεω[ς
```

'The consulship of our lords Constantius Augustus for the 4th
time and Constans Augustus for the 3rd time, Hathyr 25.

Aurelius Comes son of Harmogis, from the village Techthy of the
Diopolite nome, to Aurelius Ptolemaios son of Pachoumis, former
magistrate of Tentyra, greeting. I acknowledge that I have received
from you and have had measured out a loan of three and five-sixths
artabs of wheat, = 3⅚ art., and these I shall return to you promptly
at the time of the harvest of the auspiciously approaching sowing
of the 6th indiction in grain by the measure of Pha . . . without any
dispute. (You) shall have right of execution upon me and all my
property until repayment . . .'

4 Κόμης: the first certain papyrological instance of the name in this spelling. Of the examples cited in the *Onomasticon*, that in P. Athens 46.19 is partly restored, and the others are not names but the title 'count'. — In *Prel. Rep.* p. 12 it was stated that this man was "almost certainly" a monk because the name of a presbyter (not monk) in **77**.16 was at that time read as Κόμ[ης. Cf. note there.

Τεχθύ: cf. the Herakleopolite village Τεχθώ. This is the first mention of the locality, unless Τεχθ(ύ) rather than Τεχθ(ώ) is to be read in P. Erl. 80.89.

12 The sixth indiction referred to is 347/8 A.D.

12-3 ἐν] κόκκῳ: the phrase is found again only in P. Lond. IV 1404.23. Loans and receipts for σίτου κόκκου or σίτου καθαροῦ κόκκου are known (cf. P. Mert. I 47.4, P. Michael. 44.11, P. Mich. XIII 670.9), and a land lease specifies that rent be so paid (P. Michael. 60.10); in addition, P. Collect. Youtie 93.7 records a sale of λαχανοσπέρμου καθαροῦ κόκκου. The last instance shows that κόκκου in these passages does not refer to darnel, but in some way describes the condition of the product to be delivered. The editor of P. Lond. IV 1404 suggests that ἐν κόκκῳ refers to threshed as opposed to unthreshed wheat (10 n.).

18 I take Φα . [to be the name of the man whose measure was to be used.

65. DEED OF SURETY

VII 4ᵉ   7 × 16 cm.   7 October (?) A.D. 348

Aurelius Melas promises under oath to the chairman of a city council which can no longer be identified that he will guarantee the appearance of one Aurelia (?) Theodora whenever he is called upon to do so. For a bibliography on such documents see O. Montevecchi, *La papirologia* (Torino, 1973) 192-3. The back is blank.

→   [± 12]ωνι ἐνάρχῳ προέδρῳ
        [± 13]β′ Αὐρήλιος Μέλας
        [± 13]οσ[. . .] χαίρειν.
        [ὁμολογῶ ὀμνύ]ς τὴν θείαν καὶ οὐράνιον
5   [τύχην τῶν δεσπ]οτῶν ἡμῶν αἰωνίων
        [Αὐγούστων ἐγγ]υᾶσθαι μονῆς καὶ ἐμφα-
        [νείας Αὐρηλίαν (?)] Θεοδώραν Μαξίμου
        [μητρὸς ± 6 ἥ]ν καὶ παραστήσω ὁπόταν
        [ἐπιζητῆται ἄνευ πάσ]ης ἀντιλογίας.

10 [ἐὰν δὲ μή, ἔνοχος εἴην τ]ῷ θείῳ ὅρκῳ
    [καὶ τῷ ἐπηρτημένῳ τούτῳ] κινδύνῳ.
    [κύριον τὸ χειρόγραφον] ἁπλοῦν γραφὲν
    [± 7 ἐξεδόμην σ]οι πρὸς ἀσφάλιαν,
    [καὶ ἐπερωτηθεὶς ὡμο]λόγησα.
15 [ὑπατείας Φλαυίου Φιλίππ]ου τοῦ λαμπροτάτου
    [ἐπάρχου τοῦ ἱεροῦ πραιτωρί]ου καὶ Φλαυίου Σαλιᾶ
    [τοῦ λαμπροτάτου μαγίστρου ἱππέ]ων, Φαῶφ[ι] ι΄.

— — — — — — —

'To NN, current chairman ... Aurelius Melas ... greeting.
I acknowledge, swearing by the divine and heavenly fortune of our
lords the eternal Augusti, that I stand surety for the presence and
availability of Aurelia (?) Theodora, daughter of Maximus and NN,
whom I shall present whenever she is required, without any dispute.
Otherwise may I be subject to the divine oath and the danger bound
therewith. The note of hand ... I have given to you for security in a
single copy ... is valid, and in response to the formal question I so
declared.

Consulship of Flavius Philippus, *clarissimus praefectus sacro prae-
torio*, and Flavius Salia, *clarissimus magister equitum*, Phaophi 10 (?).'

2 β΄: e.g., restore υἱῷ NN] (δευτέρου).

3]ος may be the ending of Melas' patronymic or metronymic.
If so, nothing was written between these letters and χαίρειν.

7 Αὐρηλίαν (?): at this date only the names Flavia and Aurelia
need be considered likely. As an Aurelius was sufficient guarantee
for the appearance of this person, the probability that she herself
belonged to the Flavii, who had a higher standing, is extremely
slight. See in general J. G. Keenan, *ZPE* 11 (1973) 33-63 and 13
(1974) 283-304.

11 For the restoration cf. e.g. P. Leipz. 46.17. The commoner
expressions τῷ περὶ τούτου κινδύνῳ and τῷ ἐπηρτημένῳ περὶ τούτου
κινδύνῳ are respectively too short and too long.

12-3 Possibly ὁ] ἁπλοῦν γραφὲν | [τῇ ἐμῇ χειρὶ ἐξεδόμην (Brussels
MS). One might also think of simply ἁπλοῦν γραφὲν, | [ὃ καὶ ἐξεδόμην,
though that is rather short for the lacuna in l. 13.

66. LETTER FROM PATESE TO ABARAS

VII 5ᶜ + 6ᶜ   9 × 23.7 cm.   4th cent. A.D.

A business letter, mostly concerned with sheep and wool, written
in reasonably good Greek in a fluent but not especially elegant

hand. A photograph taken when the cover of the codex was first opened has been useful in reading some places which were damaged when the cartonnage was separated. The back is blank.

→　　　τῷ ϗ[υ]ρίῳ [μου ἀδελ-]
　　　φῷ ’Αβαρᾶτι Πα-
　　　τέσε　　ἐν Κ(υρίο)υ
　　　χαίρειν
5　　πρ[ο]ηγουμένως προσ-
　　　αγορεύω σε. σπούδασον
　　　κεῖραι τὰ πέντε ἐρ[. . .]
　　　Κάρια ἐριδίων καὶ ἄφες
　　　παρὰ σοὶ ἕως ἂν καταλά-
10　βω σε. σπ[ο]ύδασογ μὴ
　　　πωλῆσαι ἀπ’ αὐτῶν ἕως
　　　ἂν καταλάβω σε, ἐπειδή-
　　　περ οὐ δύναμαι ἐλθεῖν
　　　νυνὶ διὰ τὴν ταραχὴν
15　τῶν τειρώγ[ων. σ]πούδα-
　　　σον λαβεῖν τὸ ἐγίδιον
　　　καὶ τὸ προβάτιον ἀπὸ τοῦ
　　　ποιμένος ἡγίκα ἂν κεί-
　　　ρῃς τὰ ἕτερα, καὶ τὸ ἀργύ-
20　ρ[ι]ον λαβεῖν ἀπὸ τοῦ ’Ιω-
　　　άνου [π]ερὶ τοῦ ὄνου ὃν {πε}
　　　πέπ[ρα]ϗα Πεκυσίῳ, καὶ
　　　[λ]αβε[ῖν ἀ]πὸ Παφῷβ τὸ ἀρ-
　　　[γύριον], τοῦτ’ ἔστιν παρὰ
25　[. . . . . . .], καὶ λάβε ἀπὸ τοῦ
　　　[. . . . . .] . [.]ου τὰ Μακαρίου
　　　[　　　 ἐρ]ρῶσθαί σε εὔχομαι
　　　[πολλοῖς χρό]νοις.

---

3 ενϗυ　8 ϗαί: ϗ corrected from α　16 αἰγίδιον　17 προβάτιον: π corrected.

‘To my lord brother Abaras, Patese, greeting in the Lord. First and foremost I greet you. Be sure to shear the five Carian . . . of wool, and keep them with you until I meet you; make sure not to sell any of them until I meet you, since I am not able to come at present because of the disturbance of the recruits. Make sure to

take the goat and the sheep from the shepherd whenever you sheer
the rest, and to take the money from John in the matter of the
donkey that I sold to Pekysios, and to take the money from Paphob,
that is, from . . . And take Makarios's . . . from the . . . I pray for
your health for many years.'

2   The name 'Ἀβαρᾶς is new, but ''Ἄβαρος is found in the *NB*
and *Onomasticon*.

2-3   Πατέσε: a hitherto unattested variant of Πατῆσις or Πετεῆσις.

7-8   At first sight P. Princ. III 155 R.6 seems to suggest ἐρ[ικὰ] |
Κάρια, which would presumably mean 'Carian measures of wool',
but L. C. Youtie's revision of the text in *ZPE* 23 (1976) 120ff.
leaves no possibility of a parallel here, and no 'Carian measure' is
known: *WB* I s.v. κάριον records such a term, but it is wrongly
abstracted from δισκάριον, actually derived from δίσκος. Possibly
ἐρ]ίφια] | Κάρια, 'sheer the Carian goats of their hair', though the
construction with the genitive is odd.

14-5 In the lack of a precise date it seems hopeless to try to
connect this disturbance among the recruits with a known historical
event. It is further unclear whether one should deduce from this
statement that Patese had some official connection with the army,
or whether he means that travel had become unsafe because of
marauding troops.

21   ὄν {πε}: or ὄνπε<ρ>.

27   It is uncertain whether a word should be supplied before
ἐρ]ρῶσθαι, as τὰ Μακαρίου (26) could by itself mean 'Makarios'
things'.

67. LETTER

VII 7ᶜ   14.5 × 22.5 cm.   4th cent. A.D.

Neither sender nor receiver of this mutilated business letter can
now be identified. A monk's dwelling of some type, if that is indeed
the meaning of μονάχιον, is mentioned in l. 8; cf. Introd. pp. 7-8.

— — — — — — — — — —

→   [. . . .]λο[
        [. . . .]ηνε[
        α[. . .]πεγ[
        ἀδελφὸς ὑπα[
5   γράψαι σοι . . [. . .] . [. . . .] ἀδελφ[. . . . .] .
        λου οπε[.] . . [. . . .] παραγένηται ἐκεῖ. δέδωκ( )

εἰς τὸ πλοῖον [τὸ]ν ὀλίγον σῖτον. ποιήσῃς
αὐτὸν μεταϰ[ομί]ζεσθαι εἰς τὸ μονάχιον διὰ
τῶν ὑμετέρω[ν] κτηνῶν καὶ θεῖναι αὐτὰ

10   εἰς σιρόν. πρόσθες ὀλίγας ἡμέρας, ἐπειδὴ
περ . . . λῳ φέρει. ἀλλ' ὅρα μὴ ἀμελήσῃς.
τοὺς παρὰ σοὶ ἀδελφοὺς ἐγὼ καὶ οἱ σὺν ἐμοὶ
πάνπολλα προσαγορεύ [[ωμ.]] 'ο'μεν. ἐρρῶσθαι
                ὑμᾶς εὔχομα[ι]

15   πολλοῖς χρόνοις.
  Back → τῷ ἀγαπητῷ [μου] ἀδελφῷ . . . . [

(l. 6) '. . . arrives there. I (?) put the small quantity of grain on the boat; make him transport it to the monk's dwelling with your asses and put it in the storage bin (*or*, vessel). Reckon a few days in addition, since he carries it . . . See to it that you are not negligent. I and those with me give many greetings to the brothers who are with you. I pray for your health for many years.

(Back) To my beloved brother . . .'

6 οπε[: apparently not ὁπό[τ]αν, but ὁπηγί[ϰ' ἄν] might do.

δέδωϰ( ): person and number of the subject are not specified. 'I (?)' in the translation above is only exempli gratia.

7 ποιήσῃς: for the jussive subjunctive see Mandilaras, *The Verb* §§ 554ff.

8 μονάχιον: apparently the first certain attestation of this word; cf. A. Lumpe, "Beiträge aus der Thesaurusarbeit: monachium (Cod. Iust. I, 2, 13)", *Mus. Helv.* 17 (1960) 228-9. It is presumably equivalent to μοναστήριον. Cf. πατριαρχεῖον for the residence of a patriarch (Du Cange, s.v.).

10 σιρόν: see pp. 7-8 with notes 16 and 17.

11-2 The Brussels MS reads ἐπειδὴ περιϰύϰλῳ φέρει and translates 'since he carries it by a circuitous route'. I have found no satisfactory parallel for the expression and it is palaeographically dubious on the photograph. The word division may be ἐπειδήπερ κτλ.

68.   LETTER FROM HARPOCRATION TO SANSNOS

VII 8ᶜ   12.5 × 24 cm.   4th cent. A.D.

This business letter is the first of eight texts in Codex VII addressed to a man named Sansnos, who, if the references are all to the same person, is elsewhere called monk (**72.**1-2) and presbyter

(**78**.15) ; he may also be mentioned in **C8** a 14 and c 2, and may be the writer of the following letter. See Introd. pp. 7-9.

An appeal to the love of Christ in l. 12 is noteworthy.

→   [τῷ] ἀγ[απ]ητῷ μου πατρὶ Σανσνῶς
          'Αρποκρατίων πλ(εῖστα) ἐν Κ(υρί)ῳ χαίρειν.
          Πέτρον τὸν ἐνοχλοῦντα τῷ ἀδελ[φῷ]
          'Αππιανῷ διὰ τοὺς περὶ Παπνού[τιον]
5   τῶν ἐκφορίων ἕνεκεν ποίησον
          ὀλίγας ἔτι ἀνασχέσθαι ἡμέρα[ς]
          ἕως ἂν καιρὸν εὕρωσι ἐλθεῖν
          πρὸς σὲ καὶ ἀπαλλάξαι τὸ
          καθ' ἑαυτούς. οὕτω γὰρ ἠξίωσαν.
10   ἀλλὰ σπούδασον, ἀγαπητέ, παρά[στης]
          τῷ ἀδελφῷ. οὕτω γὰρ πρέπε[ι]
          τῇ ἐν Χρηστῷ σου ἀγάπῃ.
          εἰ δὲ ἀβαρές σοί ἐστιν, περιποίη[σον]
          ἡμῖν ἀχύρου ἀγώγια δέκα κ[αὶ]
15   πέμψον ἡμῖν ἐκ πόσων π[ι-]
          πράσκεται. προσαγορεύω
          [πάν]τας τοὺς ἀδελφοὺς μεθ' ὧν [εἰ.]
                       ἐρρωμέν[ον]
                       καὶ εὐθυμο[ῦντα]
20   διὰ τέλους σ[ε]
                       φυλάξειεν[

———   ———   ———   ———

Back: → τῷ ἀγαπητῷ μ[ου] πατρὶ Σα[νσνῶτι]
                       'Αρποκρα[τίων]

1 Σανσνῶτι (cf. note ad loc.)   2 πλ', κω   5 τῶν added in left margin
12 Χριστῷ.

'To my beloved father Sansnos, Harpocration, very many greetings in the Lord. Make Peter, who is harassing brother Appianus through Papnoutios' people in the matter of the rents, desist for a few more days until they find opportunity to come to you and settle their problem; for so they have requested. But be diligent, beloved, and come to the assistance of the brother; for thus it behooves your charity in Christ. If it is not burdensome to you, contrive to obtain for us ten loads of chaff and inform us of the

selling price. I greet all the brothers with whom you are. May (God?)
keep you in health and good spirits continually.

(Back) To my beloved father Sansnos, Harpocration.'

1 Σανσνῶς: the name is also left undeclined in **69**.17 and should
perhaps so be restored in the address of this text, l. 22.

4 In *Prel. Rep.* p. 13 it was suggested that this Papnoutios may
have been the οἰκονόμος of Pachomius; cf. above, Introd. p. 10
n. 21.

12 Χρηστῷ: this misspelling of Χριστῷ is common throughout
the Byzantine period (cf. e.g. Blass-Debrunner-Rehkopf, *NT
Grammatik* § 24). G. M. Browne informs me that in Coptic the
opposite error (ΧΡΙCΤΟC, or even ΧC, for χρηστός) is sometimes
found.

21f. Supply [ὁ Θεός, or perhaps [ἡ θεῖα πρόνοια.

22 Cf. 1 note.

69. LETTER FROM SANSNOS TO APHRODISIOS

VII 9ᶜ   13 × 25.5 cm.   4th cent. A.D.

A letter concerning various agricultural matters, written with
such indifferent use of spelling and grammar that the sense of some
passages is doubtful. The back is blank. For the correspondents cf.
Introd. pp. 8-9.

```
  →        τῷ ἀγαπυτῷ ἀδε[λφῷ 'Αφροδισίῳ]
           Σανσνῶς ἐν Κυρίῳ χ[αίρειν.]
           καθὼς ἐξῦλθας ἀφ' ὑμῶ[ν πρὸς]
           τὰ πεδία χωρὶς τρωφῆ[ς κ]αὶ σύ,
     5     'Αφροδίσιος, ὅτι πέμψομεν αὐτοῖς
           τροφύν, οὐδὲν ἔπεμψας αὐτοῖς.
           καὶ σύ, 'Αφροδί<σι>ος, ὁμολόγυσας
           ὅτι ὑπά`γ'ωμεν διτομεῖ τὰ πρόβα[τα]
           καὶ τὰ ἐγίδια. νῦν οὖν οὐδὲν ἔπεμ-
    10     ψας τοῖς πεδίας. καὶ πάλιν ἔγρα[ψα]
           ἅπαξ ἔπεμψας πρὸς σέ.
           ἐζύτησα παρὰ τοὺς ποιμένας
           περὶ τῶν κτηνῶν, καὶ εἶπαν
           οἱ ποιμένος ὁμολόγυσαν
    15     ὅτι οἱ <ἔ>χοντες τὰ πρόβατα
           καὶ τὰ θρέματα αὐτοὶ πλυρῶσιν.
```

καὶ ἐζύτησα παρὰ Σανσνῶς
ποιμένος ὅτι πῶς ποιοῦμεν
περὶ τῶν θραμάτων, καὶ εἶπαν
20   Σανσνῶς ὅτι ὀλοιπάσδυ πρόβατα
καὶ ἐγίδια, καὶ ἔδωκα αὐτοῖς
εἴκοσι θαρις. οὐδὲν ποιοῦμεν.
περὶ τὸ ἰδίοις πέμψον μοι καὶ
μάθω. καὶ ἀσπάζομεν Ἀρακλῦς
25   καὶ τοῖς ἀδελφοῖς καὶ τὰ τέκνα
Ἀρακλῦς.

ἐρ[ρ]ῶσθ[αί σε]
[εὔχομαι]
[πολλοῖς χρόνοις.]

1 ἀγαπητῷ   3 ἐξῆλθες, ἡμῶν   4 παιδία, τροφῆς   5 Ἀφροδίσιε
6 τροφήν   7 Ἀφροδίσιε, ὡμολόγησας   9 αἰγίδια   10 παιδίοις
11 ἔπεμψα or πέμψας   12 ἐζήτησα, τῶν ποιμένων   14 ποιμένες, ὡμολόγησαν or
ὁμολογοῦντες   16 θρέμματα, πληροῦσιν or πληρῶσιν   17 ἐζήτησα, Σανσνῶ-
τος   19 θρεμμάτων, εἶπε   20 ἐλοιπάσθη   21 αἰγίδια   23 τῶν ἰδίων or
τοῦ ἰδίου   24 Ἀρακλῦς, l. acc.   25 τοὺς ἀδελφούς   26 Ἀρακλῦς, l. gen.

'Sansnos to his beloved brother Aphrodisios, greeting in the Lord. As you too left us for the lads without food, Aphrodisios, because we shall send the food, you sent them nothing. You too, Aphrodisios, agreed that we should bring the sheep and goats down . . . Well now, you have sent nothing for the lads. And I wrote once again sending for you. I enquired of the shepherds about the animals, and the shepherds agreed that the men who have the sheep and lambs will pay themselves. And I enquired from Sansnos the shepherd how we are managing in regard to young animals. He said we have sheep and goats left, and I gave him twenty . . . We are doing nothing. Send to me about our own (affairs? people?) for my information. We greet Haraklys and the brothers and the children of Haraklys. I pray for your health for many years.'

2-10   If I understand these lines correctly, Aphrodisios had failed to bring food for the παιδία because he understood that Sansnos and his friends were to do that, whereas Sansnos is of the opinion that Aphrodisios should have brought food too because of the agreement concerning the sheep and goats (7-9), which presumably caused extra work for all concerned. In the Brussels MS it was suggested that εἶπες or a similar verb has fallen out after Ἀφροδίσιος in l. 5.

In that case the complaint would be that Aphrodisios had not kept his word.

2 ἐξῦλθας, l. ἐξῆλθες: for other instances of the interchange of η and υ, frequent in this text, see Gignac, *Phonology* 264-5. For the verb ending cf. Mandilaras, *The Verb* § 317(6).

5 Ἀφροδίσιος: nom. for voc. Cf. Kühner-Gerth II.1 47, 2; Blass-Debrunner-Rehkopf, *NTGrammatik* § 147; Mayser II.1 55, 2.

8 ὑπά'γ'ωμεν: of animals usually means 'yoke', but that is clearly unsuitable for sheep and goats, so I suppose it means simply 'bring them down'.

διτομεῖ might mean 'separately', though the word has not previously occurred. In this text a misspelling of a personal name such as Διδύμη would seem possible. At the end of the line προβά[τια] might be read instead of πρόβα[τα] (so **66**.17), but ll. 15 and 20 have πρόβατα.

10-1 πάλιν . . . ἅπαξ: cf. P. Abin. 32.12, ἄλλω ἄβαξ (ἄλλο ἅπαξ). Some more similar expressions are collected in **70**.12 n.

The parallel with ll. 13-4, εἶπαν . . . ὁμολόγυσαν (= ὡμολόγησαν) suggests that the scribe intended to write ἔγραψα . . . ἔπεμψα with the sense 'I wrote and sent for you'.

16 πλυρῶσιν: one might interpret this form either as πληροῦσιν or πληρῶσιν, in both cases with future meaning; cf. Mandilaras, *The Verb* §§ 214ff., 541.

17 Σανσνῶς: similarly undeclined in **68**.1.

22 θαρις: the simplest explanation phonologically is θαρρῆς as jussive subjunctive (Mandilaras § 554), 'have no fear: we are doing nothing' (against your interests, without consulting you, etc.). If it is felt that a noun object of ἔδωκα (21) should be seen in this word, I have nothing better to offer than the suggestion of the Brussels MS, θαλλία, comparing P. Bala'izah II 191.4 (ΘΑΛΛΙC).

23-4 πέμψον μοι καὶ μάθω: καί = ἵνα; cf. Blass-Debr.-Rehk. § 442.3.

24 and 26 Ἀρακλῦς: not in *NB* or *Onomasticon*. Cf. Ἡρακλῆς.

70. LETTER FROM CHENOPHRES TO PHENPSETYMES

VII 10ᶜ   10.5 × 25 cm.   4th cent. A.D.

A badly spelled letter with some interesting colloquial language, three new names and a new word.

→   [τῷ ἀγαπητῷ μου ἀ]δελφῷ Φεγ[ψε-]
            [τύμη Χενοφρῆς] ἐν Κ(υρί)ῳ χαίρει[ν.]

[προηγουμένως σ]ε προαγορεύ[ω]
[καὶ τοὺς ἐν οἴκ]ῳ κατὰ ὄν[ο-]
5   [μα   c. 13   ]α ὄσπριον
  [.........].[.....] καὶ λαχ[ά-]
  νου ἀρτάβας τρῖ[ς] ὕμισέ μοι
  καὶ ἀργυρίου τάλαντα δύο. ἀπ[ο-]
  [δ]όσῃς 'αὐτὰ' Πεβῶτος {σ} ἥνα ἀπο-
10   φέρι μοι αὐτά. ἐὰν δὲ μὴ
  ἀποδόσῃς αὐτά, ἀπετόσῃ[ς]
  τὸν ναῦλον δύο ἄπαξ. νῦγ
  ἐμέλησην τὴν προθησ-
  μία<ν>, ἀλλὰ ἀπόστιλόν μο[ι]
15   τὰ ὄσπρεον ἐπ<ὶ> τάχιον.
  καὶ φιλοπόνησον τὴν
  Βοάις καὶ θάλπισον τὴν
  θυγατέρα αὐτῆ<ς>. δῖξον
  Πεβῶτος 'τὸν υἱῷ μου' τὴν Βοάις.
20   ἐρρῶσθαί σε εὔχο-
      μαι πολλοῖς χρόνοις.

Back→   [Φεν]ψετύμης Χ παρὰ Χενοφρῆς

4-5 ὄνομα   7 τρεῖς ἥμισυ   9-10 Πεβῶτι ἵνα ἀποφέρῃ   11 ἀποδώσῃς,
ἀποδώσεις   13 ἀμέλησον (?), προθεσμίαν   14 ἀπόστειλον   15 τό   17
Βοάιν   18 δεῖξον   19 Πεβῶτι τῷ, Βοάιν

'Chenophres to my beloved brother Phenpsetymes, greeting in the Lord. First and foremost I greet you and those in your household by name . . . mixed produce . . . and three and one-half artabs of vegetables to me, and two talents of silver. Give them to Pebos so that he may bring them to me; if you do not give them, you will pay the freight charge twice. Now pay no attention to the deadline (?), but send me the produce as quickly as possible. Look after Boais and be nice to her daughter. Point out Boais to my son Pebos. I pray for your health for many years.

(Back): Phenpsetymes, from Chenophres.'

1-2 Φεν[ψε|τύμη Χενοφρῆς: cf. l. 22. Neither name is recorded in *NB* or *Onomasticon*, but for the second cf. Χονοφρῆς.

5 ὄσπριον: in l. 15 the form ὄσπρεον is used, a "late spelling . . . rejected by *EM* 635.48" (*LSJ* s.v.). To judge from the entries in the *WB*, both spellings are about equally common in the papyri;

other examples of the interchange of ι and ε are listed by Gignac, *Phonology* 249ff. At this date the word means 'mixed produce', which may include grain; see P. Cair. Isid. 76.12 n. ὄσπριον is marginally preferable to ὀσπρίου, though one expects a measure to follow.

9 ἥνα for ἵνα: cf. Gignac, *Phonology* 238.

12 ναῦλον: from ναῦλος if the preceding τόν is to be taken seriously. I do not find the masculine form in papyrological lexica, but it is recorded in *LSJ*. The neuter is so much more common in Egypt, however, that one might think of reading τὸ{ν} ναῦλον.

δύο ἅπαξ 'two times': cf. P. Mich. VIII 482 = Naldini, *Cristianesimo* 1.5, ἄλλο ἅπαξ; P. Abin. 32 = Naldini 40.8, τούτω τὸ ἄβαξ, ibid. l. 12 ἄλλω ἄβαξ; P. Ryl. II 435.2, ἄλλα ἅπαξ; Wilcken, *APF* 6 (1920) 379-80; S. G. Kapsomenakis in *Münchener Beiträge* 28 (1938) 50-1.

13 ἐμέλησην, read probably ἀμέλησον: for interchange of α and ε see Gignac 278ff., for that of η and o idem p. 293. I take it that the writer fears his correspondent may claim to have no time to carry out his request and is attempting to forestall his objection; cf. in a general way P. Fay. 114.21-2, μὴ ο<ὖ>ν ληρήσῃς τὸν ἐκτιναγμόν σου. ἠμέλησας would also make sense, but while omission of the temporal augment is common (cf. Mandilaras, *The Verb* §§ 253ff.; ἐμέλησε occurs in PSI XIV 1413.5), such a misspelling at the end of the word would be phonologically inexplicable.

15 ἐπ<ὶ> τάχιον: not very satisfactory, as the phrase appears to be unparalleled. Perhaps rather ἐν τάχιον for ἐν τάχει.

17 Βοάις: not in *NB* or *Onomasticon*.

θάλπισον: from θαλπίζω, a new word based on θάλπω.

71. LETTER FROM HORION TO —ARIOS AND DORKON

VII 11ᶜ   10.6 × 20.3 cm.   4th cent. A.D.

A polite letter to two presbyters, concerning skins and dates. Cf. Introd. p. 9.

→   [   ] . ι καὶ τυχεῖν . [
           [. . . . . . θέλω] ὑμᾶς γνῶναι, γλυκ[ύτα-]
           [τοι π]ατέρες, περὶ ὧν ὑμῖν ἔγραψ[α]
           [. . . ὅ]τι χρεία ἐστίν μοι δύο δερμά[των]

5   τ̣ . . . . . ιατ . τοῦ ἀδελφο̣ῦ̣ [. . . . .] .
.[. . . . .]αυτ[.] . [̇ .] . . . . . . [
ἀξιῶ οὖν ὑμᾶς ὅπως πανταχόθε[ν]
ζητήσητε καὶ ἀγοράσητέ μοι αὐτά. δ[έομαι]
δὲ δέρματο̣ς̣ μάλα σφόδρα. ἰδοὺ ἀ[πέ-]

10   [σ]τ̣α̣[λκα] ὑμῖν δύο ἀρτάβας φοινίκ̣[ων.]
καὶ μάθε ἀπὸ τούτων τὴν τιμὴ[ν]
τῶν δύο ἀρταβῶν καὶ τῶν δύο δ[ερμά-]
των, ὅπως γράψητέ μοι καὶ ἀ[ποστεί-]
λω πάραυτ̣ω πάλιν τ̣ὸ̣ πρόλοιπας.

15   ἀσπάζομαι ὑμᾶς πάντας κατ' ὄνομα.
ἐὰν δὲ θέλητε, πέμψαι τὰ δέρματα δ[
ἐὰν δὲ μή, γράψαι με ὅπως μάθω.
ἐρρῶσθαι ὑμᾶς
εὔχ[ο]μαι ἐν Κ(υρί)ῳ.

Back: →

20   ]αρίῳ πρ(εσβυτέρῳ) καὶ Δόρ Χ κωνι πρ(εσβυτέρῳ)
π(αρὰ) Ὡρίωνος.

10 ιν in ὑμῖν corrected from ας   11 μάθετε   14 πάραυτα, πρόλοιπον
17 μοι

'. . . I want you to know, my sweetest fathers, the matters about which I wrote you . . . that I have need of two skins . . . of the brother . . . I request of you therefore that you seek everywhere and buy them for me. I am very greatly in need of a skin. Look, I have dispatched to you two artabs of dates; and learn from these people the price of the two artabs and of the two skins, so that you may write to me and I may dispatch the balance at once. I greet you all by name. If you wish, send me the skins . . . otherwise, write me so that I may know.
I pray for your health in the Lord.
(Back) To —arios, presbyter, and Dorkon, presbyter, from Horion.'

11   μάθε: one expects μάθετε. The writer may have forgotten for the moment that he is writing to more than one person, or it may be simply a scribal slip. In the latter case, μάθε < τε > should be read.

τούτων: presumably the persons who are charged with the delivery of the letter and the dates.

16-7 πέμψαι, γράψαι: for the imperatival infinitives see Mandilaras, *The Verb* §§ 756ff., esp. § 765.

16 At the end perhaps δέρματα δ[ύο] (Brussels MS), but the word order would be odd and there are other possibilities, e.g. δ[ιὰ NN].

72. LETTER FROM PROTERIA (?) TO SANSNOS AND PSAS OR PSATOS

VII 12ᶜ   10.5 × 16.4 cm.   4th cent. A.D.

A request to two monks to find some chaff that can be purchased for use as fodder. Cf. Introd. p. 7.

→	Σανσνῶτι καὶ Ψάτος
	μοναχοῖς Προτηρ[ία] χέρ(ειν).
	εἰ δυνατὸν παρ' ὑμῖν ἐστιν
	τὸ ἐραυνῆσαι ὀλίγον
5	ἄχυρον πρὸς τὴν ὑπη-
	ρεσίαν τῶν ἐμῶν κτηνῶν
	διότι ὑστεροῦσι, καὶ οὐ-
	χ εὑρίσκω ἐνταῦθα ἀγο-
	ράσαι. ἐπὴν δὲ εὕρητε,
10	πέμψατέ με ὑπὲρ τὴν
	τιμὴν ὅτι πόσον τὴν
	ἅμαξαν ἀχύρου, καὶ ἵνα
	ἔρχεται τὸ πλοῖον . . .
	[. . π]λί[στ]ας χάριτας ὑμεῖν

Back→	Προτερία Σανσνῶτι καὶ
	Ψάτος.

1 Ψάτος, l. dat.   2 μοναχοῖς: ς added above the line (?); χαίρειν   5-6 η in ὑπηρεσίαν corr. from ε   6 κτηνω̄   9 ἐπάν   10 μοι   10-11 τῆς τιμῆς   11 σ in πόσον corr. from ι; τῆ   14 πλείστας, ὑμῖν   16 Ψάτος, l. dat.

'Proteria (?) to Sansnos and Psas (*or*, Psatos), monks, greeting. If it is possible where you are, seek out a little chaff for the use of my asses, because they are short of it and I find none to purchase here. If you find some, send to me about the price, how much it is per waggon-load of chaff, and so that the boat may come . . . (so that I may express to you) the utmost gratitude. (back) Proteria (?) to Sansnos and Psas (*or*, Psatos).'

1 Πσᾶτος: the same dative is used in l. 16. In the nominative, Ψᾶς and Ψᾶτος are both found; see *NB* and *Onomasticon*.

2 Προτηρ[ία]: Προτερία in l. 15, if rightly deciphered in both places. The feminine of this name does not appear to be known elsewhere, but an Alexandrian patriarch lynched in 457 A.D. was named Προτέριος.

4 τὸ ἐραυνῆσαι: the writer appears to have contaminated two constructions, the imperatival infinitive which should appear without the article and the articular infinitive as subject of ἐστιν.

9ff. For a more grammatical enquiry about the price of chaff cf. **68**.13ff.

12-3 ἵνα | ἔρχεται: for ἵνα with the indicative cf. e.g. *LSJ* s.v. B III.

13 After πλοῖον perhaps ὅτι altered to ὦσ|[τε. After l. 14 ὁμολογήσω or the like, governing χάριτας, has been lost.

73. VII 13ᶜ (7.9 × 6.1 cm.) + 14ᶜ (1.6 × 7.5 cm.). Two adjoining fragments of a letter. One of the persons addressed may be Sansnos, but the name is badly damaged.

→   τῷ ἀγαπητῷ ἀδελφ[ῷ
         Σαγσνῶτι καὶ Ἀπο[
         το[ῦ ἀ]δελφοῦ . . . . [. .] . [

Back→   τῷ ἀγαπη[τῷ

'To my beloved brother Sansnos (?) and Apo— ... of the brother ... (back) To the beloved ...'

74. VII 15ᶜ. 5.5 × 23.5 cm. A fragmentary letter from one Peteesis. The recipient's name is lost, unless Παῆσε in l. 24 is vocative.

→   τῷ κυρίῳ μο[υ   ]
       Πετεῆσις [   ]
       ἐν πρότοις . . [εὔ-]
       χωμαι τῷ Κ(υρί)ῳ [περὶ τῆς σῆς σωτη-]
5   ρίας. προσα[   ]
       τι . [. .] . α[   ]
       του[   ]
             (4 lines almost entirely lost)

12	μεν[	]
	⟦ . . ⟧ [	]
	μ . . [	]
15	ου ταῦτα η[	]
	Πεκύσι[	πεν-]
	τήκωντα κ[	]
	σίτου ἀρταβ[	]
	εὑρίσκεις πα[	πε-]
20	ρὶ τῆς ἀπεθη[	]
	ἀρτάβης . [	δη-]
	μόσια ερ[	]
	ἔδωκεν σο[	]
	Παῆσε πραξ[	]
25	ἐριδίῳ ῳ . [	]
	ὅτι ʼδίʼδωμι χάριν [	]

Down left margin: ↓ αὐτῷ μετα [. . . .] . . . . . . παράβαλλε ἡμᾶς
Back → ἐὰν εὑρίσκεις εὐτένος ἀνθρώπος ἀπόστιλών μ[οι]
τὰ πρόβατα . [

3 πρώτοις   3-4 εὔχομαι   16-17 πεντήκοντα   24 Παῆσε: the epsilon
has either been remade or corrected from another letter   28 εὐτόνους
ἀνθρώπους ἀπόστειλον.

(Back) 'If you find sturdy fellows, send me the sheep.'

4-5   σωτη]|ρίας: or ὁλοκλη]|ρίας.
15   ου: οὔ, οὐ, or the end of a word from the preceding line.
21-2   δη]|μόσια: if the μ is correct there can hardly be any doubt
about the restoration, as the only other word in -μοσιος listed by
the Kretschmer-Locker *Rückläufiges Wörterbuch* is συνωμόσιος,
which has not so far appeared in papyri. It remains uncertain
whether the word here is an adjective or refers to δημόσια in the
sense of 'taxes'.

75.   LETTER FROM BESARION TO SANSNOS

VII 16ᶜ   6.7 × 7.6 cm.   4th cent. A.D.

Top portion of a letter including instructions that an ἀδελφός,
brother or friend of the writer, be given five artabs of wheat. The
back is blank.

→   [τ]ῷ κυρίῳ μου
         [π]ατρὶ Σανσνῶτι
         [Β]ησαρίων χαίρειν.
         [. . . .] σε δῆλα ποσο[
5   [. . . .] . ῳ ἐρχωμένῳ
         [. .] οτων σῖτον [
         [. .] . δοῦνε τῷ ἀδελφῷ
         [μο]ῦ Πρῆτ σίτου ἀρτάβα[ς]
         [π]έντε, γί(νονται) (ἀρτ.) ε
10   ] . ασ[

5 ἐρχομένῳ   7 δοῦναι

'Besarion to my lord father Sansnos, greeting . . . you clear . . .
when he comes . . . wheat . . . to give my brother Pret five artabs
of wheat, total 5 art. . . .'

4-7 Convincing supplements for these lines have not occurred
to me. If δῆλα ποιέω can be used as δῆλον ποιέω one might think of
something on the order of [θέλω] σε δῆλα ποή|[σειν] τῷ ἐρχωμένῳ|
[πρὸ]ς τὼν (l. τὸν) σῖτον [ὥστε] | [συ]γδοῦνε κτλ., 'I want you to make
it clear to the man who comes for the wheat that he is to contribute
five artabs to Pret'. There would be no insuperable palaeographic
objection to this, but it does not present the most obvious interpretation of the traces, and as the Greek is also uncertain the correct
solution may lie in some quite different direction.

76. LETTER FROM MAKARIOS TO SANSNOS

VII 17ᶜ   9.5 × 16.2 cm.   4th cent. A.D.

Fragment from the beginning of a letter the subject of which
cannot now be determined. The back contains faint traces of ink,
no longer legible.

→   [τῷ ἀγ]απητῷ υἱῷ Σανσνῶτι
         [Μα]κάριος ἐν Κ(υρί)ῳ χαίρειν.
         [. . . .] . οῦνται ἡ γυνὴ μ[
         [. . . . . .]αι εἰς Σύρου
5   [. . . . .] . μεταλ[.] ια .
                          ]υ
                          ]ων

1 υἱῷ   2 κῳ

'Makarios to his beloved son Sansnos, greeting in the Lord . . .
wife (*or*, woman) . . . to Syros's . . .'

1 Σανσνῶτι: not Σανσνῶς, though the undeclined form is sometimes used (**68**.1 n.).

2 [Μα]κάριος: J. W. B. Barns writes as follows of this text in
Prel. Rep. p. 14: "The name Macarius is so common in monastic
circles that its occurrence as that of the writer of the fragmentary
letter in VII would hardly be worth noting, were it not for the fact
that he addresses Sansnōs . . . , called 'father' or 'brother' by all his
other correspondents, as 'my son'; this suggests that [Ma]carius
here is a person of high seniority; we note that a Macarius was the
successor of Sourous as head of the monastery of Pachnoum."

There is some reason to doubt whether the monk and presbyter
Sansnos (assuming that these are in fact one person and identical
with the Sansnos here) was a member of a Pachomian organization
(cf. Introd. p. 7), but he could of course have recognized a particularly holy man within that organization as his spiritual superior
nonetheless. But the term "son" may mean nothing more than that
Sansnos was strikingly younger than Macarius; or, indeed, that he
was his son.

3 -οῦνται is presumably the ending of a verb of which the sub-
jects are ἡ γυνή and something lost in lacuna. The construction of
ll. 3-4 may have followed the general lines of [διαν]ροῦνται ἡ γυνή
μ[| [καὶ NN ἔρχεσθ]αι εἰς Σύρου, but if ἔρχεσθ]αι was the verb used
in l. 4 I can think of no name short enough to have preceded it.
The word after γυνή may be the name of the woman or her husband,
or the pronoun μ[ου].

4 εἰς Σύρου: i.e., to Syros's home or to a place called Syrou.
There was a Σύρου χωρίον in the Fayum (*WB* III 330), but that will
hardly be meant here.

77. LETTER FROM ZACCHEOS, COM—, AND PECHENEPHNIBIS TO SANSNOS

VII 18ᶜ + 19ᶜ   (18) 5.2 × 17.1 cm.   4th cent. A.D.
                       (19) 6.2 × 20.5 cm.

Two fragments of a letter to Sansnos from three presbyters,
concerning among other things the removal of some wood or brush
and the introduction of some persons who had been recommended

by a bishop. It seems very probable that Sansnos, whom the presbyters address as ἀδελφός, is the Σανσνῶς πρεσβύτερος of **78**.15, if not also the monk of **72**.1-2; cf. **68** introd. VII 18 contains the left side of the letter, VII 19 the right; a strip in the middle has been lost. Cf. Introd. p. 6, n. 13.

```
→        [                           ] .
         [                           ] . ε
         . [ . . ] . ρα [ . . . . . . . . . . . . . . ] . . . . ἀδελ-
         φοῖς ἡμῶ[ν . . . . . . . . . . . ] . ἐνεγυήθη
5        παραγεν[ήσεσθαι ἕνεκεν τ]ῆς ἐκκοπῆς
         ὀλίγων . [ . . . . . . . . . . ] θωγ συνέσ-
         τησεν α[ὐτοὺς ἡμῖν] διὰ γραμμάτων
         ὁ πατὴρ ἡμ[ῶν ὁ . . . . ] ς ἐπίσκοπος ἵνα
         μὴ ἀμ[ελήσῃς προ]σδέξασθαι αὐτοὺς
10       καὶ ἵνα ὁ [ . . . . . . . Βη]σαρίων τὸ πλοῖον
         ἀνενόχ[λητον ἔχῃ. π]ροσαγορεύομεν
         πάντας το[ὺς παρὰ σοὶ (?) ] ἀδελφοὺς κατ' ὄνομα.
                    [ἐρρῶσθαί] σε εὐχόμεθα
                    [πολλ]οῖς χρόνοις,
15                            ἄδελφε.
```

back → [τῷ ἀγαπητῷ] ἀδελφῷ Σανσνῶτι Ζακχέος καὶ Κόμ[καὶ]
17   Πεχενεφγῖβις πρεσ[βύτεροι].

'. . . our brothers . . . he (?) was put under surety to be present to cut down a few . . . Our father, the . . . bishop, recommended them to us in a letter, so be not negligent in receiving them, and let . . . Besarion keep the boat undisturbed. We greet by name all the brothers who are with you (?). We pray for your health for many years, brother.

(Back) Zaccheos, Com—, and Pechenephnibis, presbyters, to brother Sansnos.'

5   The subject of ἐνεγυήθη is not expressed in the text. It may be impersonal, 'a guarantee was taken'.

7   α[ὐτούς: when John Barns described this text in *Prel. Rep.* p. 13 he stated that the commendation in this letter was for "an individual". That must go back to an earlier restoration α[ὐτόν which was later rightly abandoned (Brussels MS) because of αὐτοὺς in l. 9.

ἡμῖν]: it seems to me most probable that the presbyters are

informing Sansnos of a letter which had been written to them; the following ἵνα clauses are then to be taken imperatively (cf. Mandilaras, *The Verb* §§ 585ff.). It would also be possible to restore σοι here, followed by final clauses. That would presumably give a scolding tone to the letter: 'the reason that the bishop wrote you recommending the men was that you should receive them diligently (and you have not done so)'. The Brussels MS reads ὑμῖν here and ἀμ[ελήσητε in l. 9, following *Prel. Rep.* p. 13 ("a group of the brethren"). Only one person is mentioned in the address, however, and the singular is used in ll. 13 and 15.

8 To judge from the entries in *WB* III 400 s.v. ἐπίσκοπος the most likely adjectives for the lacuna are ἅγιος and ὅσιος. Lampe cites more examples of the former word applied to bishops than of the latter.

10 In the lacuna restore ἀδελφός, μοναχός, ἴδιος ἡμῶν, or the like.

12 το[ὺς παρὰ σοὶ (?)] ἀδελφούς: the restoration is taken from **67.**12-3, τοὺς παρὰ σοὶ ἀδελφοὺς ἐγὼ καὶ οἱ σὺν ἐμοὶ πάμπολλα προσαγορεύομεν (cf. also Naldini, *Cristianesimo* nos. 19.9, 20.9, 28.7, 29.13 etc.), but there are other possibilities as well. The Brussels MS suggests ἡμετέρους.

16 Ζαχχέος: usually spelled Ζαχαῖος or Ζαχέος. Barns has pointed out that a man of this name was "one of Pachomius's most responsible subordinates" (*Prel. Rep.* p. 14).

Κομ[:the length of the name to be restored cannot be accurately estimated. The *NB* and *Onomasticon* together list 36 masculine names which begin with Κομ-; of these, Κόμων appears to be the most common. The suggestion on p. 12 of *Prel. Rep.* that this person may be the same as the Aurelius Comes of our **64.**4 is based on an earlier restoration Κόμ[ης here. Even if that should be correct the identification would be doubtful.

17 Πεχενεφυῖβις: not in *NB* or *Onomasticon*.

πρεσ[βύτεροι rather than πρεσ[βύτερος because that form would refer to Pechenephnibis alone, whereas Zaccheos too is called a presbyter in **78.**15.

78. LETTER FROM ZACCHEOS TO SANSNOS

VII 20^c + 21^c   (a) 7 × 6 cm.   4th cent. A.D.
    (b) 10.3 × 16.5 cm.

Two non-contiguous fragments of a letter introducing one Herakleios to Sansnos. For the correspondents see **77**; cf. Introd.

p. 8. A bibliography on such letters of introduction is given by
O. Montevecchi, *La papirologia* (Torino, 1973) 243.

→ τ[ῷ ἀγαπητῷ μου ἀδελφῷ Σανσνῶτι]
Ζακχέος ἐν Κ(υρί)ῳ χ[αίρειν.]
ἐν πρώτοις ἀναγκαῖο[ν ἡγησάμην]
προσειπεῖν σου τὴν ἔμ[φυτον ἀγά-]
5 πην, ἔπειτα καὶ γράφειν [σοι ἵνα]
προσδέξῃ τὸν ἀδελφὸν [ἡμῶν]
Ἡράκλειον παρ[
προ[. . .] . [

— — — — —

. [
10 . [
συνεσ[
[ἐρρῶσθαί σε εὔ-]
                           χομαι,
                           ἀγαπητὲ ἄδελφε.
                    10 cm. blank.
Back→
15 τῷ ἀγαπητῷ [μου ἀδελφῷ] Σανσνῶτι πρεσβυτέρῳ Ζαχέος πρεσβύτ[ερος.]

'Zaccheos to my beloved brother Sansnos, greeting in the Lord.
Before all I have thought it necessary to address your inborn love,
and then to write you that you may receive our brother Herakleios
. . . I pray for your health, beloved brother.
(Back) Zaccheos presbyter to my beloved brother Sansnos
presbytei.'

4-5 τὴν ἔμ[φυτον ἀγά]|πην: cf. P. Cair. Masp. I 67020v.1.

11-2 I have printed the minimum restoration, but as other texts
from this codex use a lengthier closing formula one should perhaps
rather think of something on the order of ἐρρῶσθαί σε | πολλοῖς
χρόνοις εὔ]|χομαι. For the word order in that case cf. e.g. P. Herm.
Rees 4 = Naldini, *Cristianesimo* 38.11-3. Still longer formulations,
as in P. Lugd-Bat. XI 26 = Naldini 13.21-4, are also possible.

79. LETTER

VII 23ᶜ + 24ᶜ   (23) 3.2 × 15.5 cm.   4th cent. A.D.
                     (24) 2.8 × 1 cm.

Two fragments from the center of a letter which begins with a request for some meal, whether for the writer or for some other person. The concluding half consists of greetings to various people. The back is blank.

$\rightarrow$

]ονδα Παθε[
]   χα[ίρειν.
] Παθερμοῦθι[
] χρείας ἕνεκε[ν
5   ] περιποίησον [
] ἀλεύρου ἀκαν[
ὅ]τι χρείαν ἔχ[
]τηδεως ποι[
]ων καὶ τὴν α[
10   ἀδ]ελφοὺς ἀσπ[άζομαι
] κατ' ὄνομα α[
ἀσπάζο]μαι Μαιουμ[
ἀσπά]ζομαι τοὺς α[
]θιν τὸν ἀδ[ελφ
15   ο]υς κατ' ὄνομ[α
]   ἐρρῶ[σθαί σε]
[εὔ]χομαι π[ολλοῖς]
[χρόνοις] ἐν Κ(υρί)ῳ,
[ἀ]γαπητέ [μου ἀδ]ελφ[ε .]

12 ο in Μαιουμ[corrected from ι

Except for the concluding 'I pray for your health in the Lord for many years, my beloved brother' the text is too mutilated for translation.

1   As the writers of the letters in this codex elsewhere put their own names after that of the addressee we should probably print]ονδα as dative, followed by a patronymic or the name of the writer.

6   The obvious restoration is ἀλεύρου ἀκαν[θίνου, 'acacia flour', but the substance is not otherwise known and it is not clear to me from the description of the uses of the acacia in *RE* I 1159-62 from what part of the plant flour would be made nor what purpose it would serve: the likeliest would perhaps be a powder of hard gum for medicinal use (cf. C. Preaux, *CE* 31, 1956, 140; L. C. Youtie, *ZPE* 23, 1976, 126). One can, however, think of supplements which

render this speculation idle: e.g., περιποίησον [ἡμῖν | ὀλίγα μέτρα] ἀλεύρου· 'Ακαν[θὼν | γὰρ λέγει ὅ]τι χρείαν ἔχ[ει αὐτοῦ, 'Get a few measures of flour for us; for Akanthon says that he needs it'.

12   The only name beginning Μαιουμ- in *NB* or *Onomasticon* is Μαιουμᾶς (one occurrence, SPP XX 147.6).

14   ]θιν: or]ᾳ̣ιν.

19   ἀ]γαπητέ is on a separate fragment (VII 24), and it is not certain that it should be positioned here.

80. LETTER

VII 27ᶜ + 28ᶜ + 29ᶜ   (a) 4 × 8.5 cm.   4th cent. A.D.
                                (b) 2.8 × 4 cm.
                                (c) 2.5 × 4 cm.

Three fragments of a letter, the first from the top, the third from the end, and the second someplace in between. Apart from a few isolated words and phrases only the concluding wish for the addressee's health is now intelligible.

```
(a) →                     ] .              [
                          ]ιωμ . . . . . . .[
                          ] . ις καὶ καλ . [
                          ]ωνις πολλ[
5                      γινώ]σκιν σε θέλ . [
                          ] χρίαν[
                          ]ρευσωγ[
                            ]ννιο[
                          ]τῷ ἀδελφ[
                        —    —    —    —
(b)
10                            ] . [
                          ]πϱδοσι̣[
                          [σινιταυ[
                          ] . ἐπιδὴ δ[
                          ] . ενιου[
15                        ]δῳ[
                        —    —    —    —
(c)                     —    —    —    —    —    —
                          ]μοι[
                          ]ω καὶ . [
```

] . ννι (2nd hd.) ἐρ[ρῶσθαί]
 ϲε εὔχ[ομαι]

— — — — —

Back→
20   ἀπ(όδος) Π . . τ[

1   The supposed ink trace may be only a smudge.
3   After καλ either τ or π.
5   θέλω or θέλο[μεν.
11 Probably a form of ἀπόδοσις or ἀποδίδωμι.
20 That is, 'deliver to P—' (the addressee).

81. LETTER

VII 30ᶜ   5.6 × 11.5 cm.   4th cent. A.D.

The lower portion of a letter mentioning a deposit and requesting
the addressee not to abandon a παῖς who has apparently fallen into
difficulties. The back is blank.

— — — — —

↓   ]ατῳ
                     ]αυτα ἀγορ[
                     ]αταυ . .
                     ] . παρα
5   ]υτωτασι
       . [. . .] . [. . .]η ἀδελ-
       φη . . [. .] . . . ς
       ἃ παρεθέμην σοι.
       ἀλλὰ μὴ ἀπολ[εί-]
10   ψῃς τὸν παῖ-
       δα ἐν τωσούτῳ.
                     [ἐρ]ρῶσθαί
                     [σ]ε εὔχομαι
                     [κύ]ριέ μου πολ-
15   [λοῖς] χ[ρόνοις.]

11 τοσούτῳ

(ll. 8ff.) '. . . which I deposited with you. But do not abandon the
lad in such a situation. I pray for your health for many years, my
lord.'

6-7 ἡ ἀδελ|φή or τ]ῇ ἀδελ|φῇ. If the latter, the thought may have
been 'give so-and-so's sister the things that I deposited with you'.
 9 The end of the line is obscured by an ink blot.

82. ACCOUNTS

VII 31ᶜ   9.8 × 6.9 cm.   4th cent. A.D.

One side of this papyrus records amounts collected in kind by
various persons, while a single line in the same hand on the other
side mentions an amount of money. I print first the more extensive
text, which is written against the fibers.

```
           ⎯    ⎯    ⎯    ⎯    ⎯    ⎯
  ↓        ] . . . α . . . . .                          [
           ] . . [ . . ] .                              [
           ] . . ε διὰ Ἐπωνύχου καὶ Παμε . .      . [
           ] . οτου Σαχαρίου διὰ Σανεῖς πρ(  ) . [
  5        ] διὰ Σοισοιεῖς . ᾱ
           δ]ιὰ Μουσῆς . α
           δ]ιὰ Ὡρίων . ᾱ {α}
              ]αλθιβ μά(τια) ε̄
                ] . εις . ᾱ
  10          ] . μά(τια) ε̄
           ⎯    ⎯    ⎯    ⎯    ⎯    ⎯
  Col. ii
              δι' Ἀθανα[
              διὰ Σιλβα[
              διὰ Παυλε[
              διὰ Βῆκις τ[
  15          διὰ Παχούμ[ιος
              διὰ Σιεν[
           ⎯    ⎯    ⎯    ⎯    ⎯    ⎯
  Back→     ]ερ ζ ὅμοιος ἀργυρίον (τάλαντ ) . [
              6 cm. blank
```

4ff. read gen. after διά   17 ὁμοίως ἀργυρίου

3, 5-7, 9 The thing collected in these lines is represented by a
symbol which I do not recognize, ᴸ'. The Brussels MS suggests
σ(ίτου ἀρτάβη) or σ(αργάνη). It may be simply (ἀρτάβη).
 4 Σαχαρίου: usually spelled with Z.
Σανεῖς: cf. Σάνις, Σαννεύς etc.

5 Σοισοιεῖς: cf. Σοισόις in O. Tait II 1764.6.

17 The first word was probably ὑπ]ὲρ. If so, translate 'for the 6th [i.e., indiction?] likewise, (so many) talents of silver'.

83-142

Small fragments of texts from the fourth century A.D., for the most part probably remnants of personal letters.

83. VII 25ᶜ. 2.6 × 5.8 cm. There are faint traces of writing on the back as well.

→   ]τοι ἀδελφο[

84. VII 26ᶜ. 1.2 × 1.8 cm. The back is blank.

→   ] χαιρ[
         ] . ενομ[

1 Perhaps χαίρ[ειν, but there are other possibilities, such as the name Χαιρ[ήμων.

2 The first letter could be ι or ν, but not γ.

85. VII 33ᶜ. 12.7 × 5 cm. The back is blank.

→   γενα ἀπαντῆσαί σοι δι᾽ ἀγκάρας χρ[
         Παχοῦμις ᾽Απσηνᾶς
         Ψεκῆς Ψεκῆτος

1 γενα: the ending of a word from the line lost above. ἀγκάρας, if rightly read, is new. It may be a name.

2 ᾽Απσηνᾶς: not in NB or Onomasticon.

86. VII 32ᶜ. 1.4 × 4.6 cm. Back blank.

→   ]πεγρα[
         ] . ομι[
         ] . υθ . [
         ] τῆς β[

5   ]βαι[
           ] . [

— — — —

87. VII 34ᶜ. 7.4 × 2.8 cm.

                    Σιλβανῷ καὶ Πλη[
                    . . [.] . . [

— — — —

88. VII 35ᶜ. 4.4 × 1.1 cm.

— — — — --

                    ]ομένου σίτ[ου

— — —

89. VII 36ᶜ. 5 × 5.6 cm.

— — —

                    ]την[
                    ϛετ[

— — —

90. VII 37ᶜ. 2.5 × 2.9 cm.

                    ] Αὐρηλι[
                    ] ι . . . . [

— — —

91. VII 38ᶜ. 2.8 × 2.5 cm.

— — —

                    ] . . [. .] . . [
                    ] ἀδελφοι[

— — —

92. VII 39ᶜ. 1.5 × 4.5 cm.

— — —

         →   ]τιϱ . [
                    ] . ἑπτά . [
                    ] (Space for 1 line)
                    ] . ωσθ[

5   ] . σχον[
            ]ιο[

—   —

5   could also be read as εχον.

93.   VII 40ᶜ. 5.2 × 1.2 cm.

—   —   —

π]αρ' ὑμῳ[ν

—   —   —

94.   VII 41ᶜ. 2.5 × 1.2 cm. The back contains traces of two
letters.

—   —   —

→   ]ελουσ[

—   —   —

95.   VII 42ᶜ. 1.7 × 2.1 cm.

—   —   —

] Α[ὐ]ρ[
]αγαθο . [

—   —   —

The specks which appear on the plate below line 2 are not writing.

96.   VII 43ᶜ. 2.9 × 2 cm. Smudges on the back are probably not
writing.

—   —   —

] . . . . [
] επειτα α . [
] . τοπαλε[

—   —   —

2   Two possibilities are ἔπειτα α . [and ἐπεὶ τὰ α . [.

97.   VII 44ᶜ. 2.6 × 9.6 cm.

—   —   —

] . α . [
] . ειαλο[
]λα[

—   —   —

98. VII 22ᶜ. 2.5 × 1 cm.

—   —   —

→   ]θ$\underset{.}{\varsigma}$

—   —   —

99.   VII 110ᶜ. 0.5 × 3.6 cm. Text: →]$\underset{.}{\varepsilon}$[.

100.   VII 106ᶜ. 2.9 × 11.1 cm. Account. The recto contains the
ends of 9 lines, of which the following can be read: → ⁴] . ον ⁷]ιο.
On the back, in a different hand, are traces from the beginning of
8 lines. Text: ↓ ²$\underset{.}{\varsigma}$ or θ, ⁸ε[.

101.   VII 107ᶜ. 4.5 × 3.7 cm. The recto contains the letters
απο̣σχω[(i.e., ἀπόσχω[μεν *vel sim.*) and traces of a further line. On
the verso stands διοσπολ[. This may mean Diospolis, the Diospolite
nome, or a man from Diospolis; but a different word division would
give Δῖος πολ[, i.e., Dios son of Pol—, Dios the councilman
(πολ[ιτευόμενος]), or the like.

102.   VII 108ᶜ. 3 × 1.7 cm. Text: → ¹] . ιο . [²] . π̣α̣γ[.

103.   VII 109ᶜ. 4.5 × 5.6 cm. The text is written against the
fibers, the other side being blank: ↓ ¹]αρ[²] . . [³]κ . [.

104.   VII 112ᶜ. 1.8 × 4.2 cm. The text is written against the
fibers, the other side being blank: ↓ ¹] . ω [²]περιπ[. Traces of 2
more lines.

105.   VII 113ᶜ. 1.7 × 3.5 cm. Text (front): →]μεν[, one more
line. On the back are only scattered traces.

106.   VII 114ᶜ. 2.5 × 3.9 cm. Text: → ¹]γ ²] . νκω ³]πητι.

107.   VII 51ᶜ. 1.9 × 1.2 cm. Text: →]ειγ[.

108.   VII 121ᶜ. 1.5 × 2.2 cm. Text: → ¹ . του[²] . [.

109.   VII 122ᶜ. 1.3 × 2.3 cm. Upper margin preserved. Text:
→ ¹]ρο . [²]π'π [.

110.   VII 124ᶜ. 1.2 × 0.7 cm. Text: → ¹]υον[²] . ογ[.

111.   VII 125ᶜ. 0.8 × 2 cm. Text: → ¹]αλα[²] . η . [.

112.   VII 127ᶜ. 1.2 × 2.1 cm. Text: → ¹] . [²]εκπ[³].ϛου [⁴] . [.

113.   VII 128ᶜ. 1.8 × 1.1 cm. Text: →]τοι[.

114.   VII 129ᶜ. 1.5 × 1.6 cm. Text: → ¹] . [²]ωντα[. Illegible traces on the other side.

115-123 may all be fragments of a single document.

115.   VII 134ᶜ. 1.6 × 0.2 cm. Text: →] . απον[.

116.   VII 135ᶜ. 1.5 × 0.5 cm. Text: →]ταμ . . [. On the back, slight traces of one line.

117.   VII 136ᶜ. 2 × 0.3 cm. Text: →]αρατοιου[(e.g., π]αρὰ τοιού[του).

118.   VII 137ᶜ. 1.5 × 0.5 cm. Text: →]ροϛ.

119.   VII 138ᶜ. 1.6 × 0.7 cm. Text: → ¹] . . οι . . [²] . . .[.

120.   VII 139ᶜ. 1.3 × 0.7 cm. Text: → ¹] . ολλ[²] . [.

121.   VII 140ᶜ. 1.1 × 0.2 cm. Text: → ιο . [.

122.   VII 141ᶜ. 1.4 × 0.4 cm. Text: →] . εα[.

123.   VII 142ᶜ. 1.2 × 0.3 cm. Trace of one letter on the front side.

124.   VII 130ᶜ. 1.2 × 0.5 cm. Text: →]πε[. On the back are faint traces which may not be writing.

125.   VII 143ᶜ. 2.1 × 1.6 cm. Text: →] . τι[.

126.   VII 144ᶜ. 1.9 × 2.1 cm. Text (front) →] . B . [. On the back are scattered traces. It is uncertain whether the front text is Greek or Coptic.

127.   VII 145ᶜ. 4.2 × 2.3 cm. Text: → ¹]επεν . . [²]ενταυ[.

128.   VII 146ᶜ. 6 × 4.9 cm. Top margin preserved. Text: →
¹ευσα[²δι' Ωσι . [³Πανύτιος [.

129.   VII 147ᶜ. 2.2 × 1.5 cm. Text: →]νο[.

130.   VII 148ᶜ. 1.1 × 1.1 cm. Text: → ¹]αι[²]σα[³] . υσ[.

131.   VII 149ᶜ. 1.5 × 1.5 cm. Text: →]π[.

132.   VII 150ᶜ. 2 × 2.1 cm. Text: → ¹]οσ[²] . [³] . . . π . [.

133.   VII 80ᶜ. 1.5 × 1.1 cm. Text: →] . μο[.

134.   VII 152ᶜ. 1 × 1 cm. Text: →] δ(ιὰ) [. Back: traces.

135.   VII 153ᶜ. 1.5 × 0.6 cm. Text: →]ποι[.

136.   VII 154ᶜ. 1.6 × 0.7 cm. Text: →]πον . [.

137.   VII 155ᶜ. 0.9 × 1.0 cm. Text: → ¹] . [²]επα[.

138.   VII 156ᶜ. 0.7 × 0.2 cm. Text: →] . ε . [.

139.   VII 157ᶜ. 0.5 × 0.7 cm. Text: →]απ . [.

140.   VII 158ᶜ. 1 × 0.7 cm. Text: →]ο . [.

141.   VII 159ᶜ. 0.7 × 0.6 cm. Text: →]σιο[.

142.   VII 160ᶜ. 1.1 × 0.7 cm. Text: →]ε . ο[, plus traces on the
back.

In addition to the texts described above and the Coptic documents **C2-14**, the cover of Codex VII contained thirty-four tiny
fragments most or all of which were written in Greek, but which
are too mutilated for transcription.

CODEX VIII

143-4. IMPERIAL ORDINANCES (?)

John Barns has described the documents printed here as **143-4** as follows (*Prel. Rep.* p. 11): "VIII contains, besides a few scraps of letters in Greek and Coptic [**145, C15-9**], fairly extensive, though tantalizingly incomplete, remains of two texts in Greek which seem to be without an exact parallel among the papyri. They are evidently copies of imperial ordinances, applying not particularly to Egypt, but to the Empire as a whole. Their style is reminiscent of the letters of Constantine preserved in Eusebius,[1] but they are evidently concerned not with religious matters, but with administrative and fiscal abuses and reforms. They are couched in the most general terms, and there is nothing in them which points to particular occasions[2] or to the authorship of particular emperors; but the mention in one of them of *exactores* and *praepositi* [**144**(*h*).6, 16; cf. **143**(*a*).11] indicates a date after A.D. 309. I cannot identify them with any of the extant ordinances of Constantine or his immediate successors in the Roman legal codices." For the date A.D. 309 Barns refers (ibid. n. 2) to J. D. Thomas, "The Office of Exactor in Egypt", *CE* 34 (1959) 124ff., who cites P. Giess. 103r of A.D. 309 as the earliest reference to the *exactor* in Egypt.

That the texts contain directives of some nature is certain: cf. προσετάξαμεν in **143**(*a*).10, the imperatives in **143**(*b*).10, 17, (*f*).3, 13; **144**(*a*).20, and the repeated references to "our decisions" (**143**(*b*).5, **144**(*a*).4, (*h*).17; cf. (*a*).9). The authority which issued them plainly stood higher than exactors and praepositi, and while those terms can have various meanings it is most natural in this context to take the first as the nome exactors who replaced strategi in the fourth century and the second as praepositi pagi. Moreover, **144**(*h*).19, mutilated though the passage is, very probably indicates that the author(s) of these papyri ranked higher than the governors of provinces. There can hardly be any doubt that Barns is correct

---

[1 Listed by I. A. Heikel, *Die griechischen christlichen Schriftsteller der ersten drei Jahrhunderte: Eusebius Werke*, Vol. I (Leipzig, 1902) lxxi-ii.]
[2 A possible exception is **143**(*b*), which may refer to a war.]

in attributing these regulations to emperors: whether one should seek a single emperor or a group of colleagues is doubtful, as the plural which is consistently used may be a plural of majesty.

Again, as Barns reported, there is nothing in the preserved portions of the texts which seems to refer to specifically Egyptian conditions. On the other hand, there are several references to "provincials" (**143**(*b*).6, (*f*).18, **144**(*a*).24, perhaps **143**(*f*).13); and if, as seems likely, **144**(*h*).19 contains a regulation affecting various provincial governors, then the ordinances were at least in part aimed at an area larger than any one of the Egyptian provinces and may well have covered the Empire as a whole.

If these regulations affected an area wider than Egypt, that fact would disturb the terminus post quem which Barns offered, for the date of the introduction of the exactor may not have been the same in all provinces; nevertheless, the early to mid fourth century remains a reasonable date for the texts. The stylistic comparison which Barns makes with the letters of Constantine should, however, not be pressed so far as to attribute the regulations to him on those grounds, as we have not sufficient text preserved to make an accurate judgement. **143-4** use a number of recherché words and phrases, and employ the optative (**143**(*b*).17, **144**(*a*).6, 7, 9), but these are common traits in educated Greek of the period.

It is quite uncertain how many fragmentary regulations these papyri preserve, and still more so how many they contained when complete. There is no indication as to whether all the ordinances were issued at one time or even within a single reign. The subject matter of the various fragments, so far as it can still be determined, is discussed in individual introductions. It may be said in general that it is never clear what specific problem a regulation is intended to solve, nor what the solution ordered was. The texts are not well enough preserved that one could state with confidence whether this uncertainty is due to vague rhetoric in the drafting of the documents, or simply to the extremely fragmentary nature of their remnants.

143 shows a change of hand in col. ii of fragment (*f*). Portions of the text written in this second hand have therefore been printed after (*f*), but otherwise there is no indication of the relative positions of the various fragments and the order chosen for reproduction is arbitrary. A few of the pieces have been left adhering to the cover of the codex, written side up. Their removal would have damaged the cover, and as the backs of all the detached pieces except **143**(*a*) are blank this damage is unlikely to have been compensated by any scholarly gain; cf. *Prel. Rep.* p. 11 n. 3.

Revision of the texts on the originals would be desirable.

143

(*a*)   VIll 1ᶜ. 6.1 × 22.5 cm. To judge from the mentions of shamelessness (5), robbery (7), exactors (11), storehouses (14), and registers (16, 18), this fragment was concerned with fiscal reform, probably including more careful control over the warehouses where goods collected by the state were kept.

An upper margin of 4.5 cm. is preserved, and a lower of 4.3 cm. On the back is a mirror image of the first 9 lines of the Coptic text **C16**, frag. a.

```
→            ] . ἀποδ[
             ] . . υ καὶ [
             ]επειξα[
             ] τῶν λοιπ[
5        ἀνα]ισχύντων . [ . ]μβ[
         ]ἀλλ' εἰσὶν καὶ συ[κο]φά[ν]τα[ι
         ]των διαρπαξ[ . . . . . ] . . [
         ]μις ἀκριβ . [
         ] . αυτους καὶ [
10       ] προσετάξαμεν [ . . ]ω επ[
         ]ητων ἐξακτ[όρ]ων ε[
         ] . πρόφασιν ἔχε[ι γ]ὰρ κ[
         π]ολλὴ προθυμί[α . . . ] . . [
         πρ]ὸς ἄμιλλαν τὰς ἀποθήκα[ς
15       ]ωνητης ἀδικείας α . [
         ]εν ἀναγράψει ἐγ το͂ι[ς
         ] ἐνιαυτοῦ ἐπινεμησ[
         ] ἀναγραφὴ διδάξει [
         ] . τι τῷ ἔθνει ὑπ' ὄψεσι[ν
```

15 ἀδικίας

(l. 5) '. . . shameless . . . they are informers too . . . having robbed . . . exact (ly) . . . we have ordered . . . of the exactors . . . excuse; for he has . . . much zeal . . . in competition the storehouses . . . injustice . . . he shall register in the . . . year, apportion (ment) . . . register will show . . . for the province under the eyes . . .'

1   The first letter may be α. Then ἀποδ[suggests a form of ἀποδίδωμι or ἀπόδοσις, but the word division could be ἀπὸ δ[or ἀπ' ὁδ[.

3   From ἐπείγω or a compound.

4   λοιπ[ῶν, λοιπ[αζομένων or the like.

6   Perhaps simply τῶν διαρπαξ[άντων, but something like τὰ ὑπάρχοντα αὐ]τῶν διαρπάξ[αντες is also possible.

8   ἀκριβ . [: from ἀκριβής or a related word.

9   The first letter may be σ. That suggests e.g. πρὸ]ς αὐτούς or το]σαύτους.

11-2   **144**(h).16 suggests τῶν πραιποσίτων] ἢ τῶν ἐξαχτ[όρ]ων. On the exactor see J. Lallemand, *L'administration civile de l'Egypte de l'avènement de Dioclétien à la création du diocèse* (284-382) (Brussels, 1964) 118-26; J. D. Thomas, "The Office of Exactor in Egypt", *CE* 34 (1959) 124-40.

The sense of these two lines may have been 'let no-one of the praepositi or exactors do such-and-such on any pretext (with κατὰ μηδεμία]ν πρόφασιν in l. 12); for he has (e.g., sufficient salary without this, and in addition risks such-and-such a punishment)'.

13   E.g., ἔστω οὖν π]ολλὴ προθυμί[α ὑμῖ]ν, 'be therefore very zealous (to carry out your appointed tasks)'.

15   Letter spacing suggests (but does not impel) a word break between ων and η. Among the possibilities then are ἡ τῆς ἀδικείας ἀρ[χή, 'the beginning of the injustice' and ἢ τῆς ἀδικείας ἄρ[χεσθαι, 'or to begin injustice'.

16   The most obvious supplements are καθ'] ἓν ἀναγράψει ἐν τοῖ[ς λόγοις, 'he shall register in the records in detail'. The subject of the verb may be the same as that of ἔχε[ι in l. 12 (the praepositus or exactor? cf. n. there), or may have changed.

17   In this context ἐπινέμησις in the sense of 'indiction' or 'tax assessment', or a form of ἐπινέμω, seems more probable than a reference to ἐπινέμησις as forced land assignment.

18   The general idea is presumably that records kept according to this decree will accurately reflect deliveries to and from the storehouses. It seems simplest to take ἀναγραφή as the subject of διδάξει, but doubtless a construction with τῆ] ἀναγραφῆ and a different subject could also be found.

19   In view of the frequent mentions of ἐπαρχιῶται, 'provincials', in this text (listed above, p. 88), ἔθνος in the sense of 'province' (*WB* s.v. 3) seems likely.

(*b*) VIII 2ᶜ. In two parts, which join: (a) 4.7 × 18.5 cm., (b) 6 × 9 cm. (a) has not been removed from the cover, but has been photographed together with (b), which contains the ends of ll. 14-21, in the *Facsimile Edition*. A lower margin of 4.5 cm. is preserved. L. 1 may be the first line of the column.

The subject of this fragment is most unclear. Mentions of enemies (l. 14) and dangers (15) could be references to a real war, ll. 18 and 20 plainly refer to tax collection. Regulations for some sort of military levy, perhaps? On a more banal, and therefore more probable view, the decree may be aimed at rapacious officials who treat their own countrymen as if they were enemies, unmindful of the danger of punishment they thereby incur.

```
  →                      ] . . σ . [
                         ] . . . . ψα . . ασι [
                         ] . . σησεισφ . . [
                         ] . . . . ἀπο . . τῳ[
     5          ]α τῆς ἡ[μ]ετέρας κρίσ[εως
                ]ου τῶν ἐπαρχιωτ[ῶν
                ] . . τὴν μὲν τῶν [
                ] . ου λόγον ἀπαιτ[
                ]μ[ . . ] . αὐτουργήματα[
    10          ] υ φυλαττέσθω . [
                ] . . . . μων ἐχου[
                ] . . . ρῳ καὶ ἐμφυλιοι[
                ] . . ας ἑαυτῶν ὑπερ[
                ] καὶ πολεμίους τε καὶ . . . [
    15          ] . . κιγδύνους τε καὶ αμ . [
                ] πρὶν τὰς ἁρπαγὰς ποιει[
                ] . ιγ πειραθείη ἔστωσαν τα[
                ] ἐκτὸς τῆς ὡρισμένης ποσότη[τος
                ] . . μασιγ τὴν ἁρμόζουσαν ἀπεφην[
    20          ] . . . τες ἔν τε ταῖς ἀπαιτήσεσιν α[
                ]η πρρσεοικυια . [ . ]εξων τοὺς αλ[
```

(l. 5) 'our judgement . . . of the provincials . . . that of the . . . account . . . own deeds . . . intestine . . . their own . . . both enemies and . . . both dangers and . . . should be attempted, let them be . . . apart from the prescribed quantity . . . the fitting . . . both in the collections . . . the proper . . .'

5   Perhaps δι]ά.

8   At the end, a form of ἀπαιτέω, ἀπαίτησις, ἀπαιτητής, or a related word.

9   αὐτουργήματα[the only previous instance in the papyri is P. Cair. Masp. II 67244.

10   φυλαττέσθω . [or φυλαττέσθωϲ[αν: context does not show the subject, nor whether the middle or the passive sense is required. For other examples of the Attic form in -ττ- see Gignac, *Phonology* pp. 152-3.

12   ἐμφύλιοι or ἐμφυλίοι[ϲ. This is the only mention of the word in documentary papyri to date.

14   At the end, perhaps ἐχθ[ρούς.

15   A letter may have been lost between καί and αμ . [.

21   προσεοικυῖα or προσεοικυίᾳ. Two letters may be lost in the lacuna before εξων.

(*c*)   VIII 3ᶜ. 2.5 × 3.7 cm. Fragment from the bottom of a column of indeterminable context. Cf. (*d*).

— — — —

→   ]αμαιω[
          ἐ]πιμελη[
          ]ετωσκ . [
          c. 2.5 cm. blank

2   A form of ἐπιμελέω, ἐπιμελητής, or a related word, unless one should divide ἐ]πὶ μελη[.

(*d*)   VIII 4ᶜ. 4.5 × 7 cm. Fragment from the bottom of a column, possibly the same column as (*c*), but if so the relative positions of the two pieces can no longer be determined.

— — — —

→   ] . ε . [
           ]αϲ[
          ] . ων κα[
          ] . τως ει . [
5   ] . την χαρτ[
          c. 4 cm. blank

5   If την is the article τὴν or the end of an adjective modifying the following word, then only χαρτ[ηράν or one of the variant

spellings reported in *LSJ* s.v. is possible. This would then be the latest mention of the charge, on which see most recently N. Lewis, *Papyrus in Classical Antiquity* (Oxford, 1974) 135-9. But there may be no grammatical connection between χαρτ[and the preceding word.

(*e*)   VIII 5ᶜ. 2.6 × 4.1 cm.

```
   ─        ─       ─       ─
   →                      ] . α[
                      ] . ατοσα[
                      ]αι καθη[
                      ]κεκινη[
      5        ] ἐν τοῖς ἐπ[ . ]ρ[
               ]ων]] ἀνθρῳ[π

   ─        ─       ─       ─
```

(*f*)   VIII 6ᶜ + 7ᶜ. 22.8 × 11.6 cm. Adjoining fragments of two columns, the second of which is in a different hand from that of the pieces of **143** printed up to here. That this edict was intended to check the greed of certain individuals can hardly be doubted (l. 14, πλεονεξίαν), but just what legal offense it was meant to counter is not clear to me. Mentions of 'habitual evil' (9, 10), plotting (13), outrages (15), return (of what? 11), and persons who had never attempted to obtain something through the law courts (12) may point to informers or abuse of the law in connection with debts.

```
   ─        ─       ─       ─
   →                      ]ται . ρ . ρτι . [
                      ] . ων ʽμʼέμψεως γα[
                      ]αι ὁπλἱζέʼσθω κατὰ τῶ[ν
      ]σαν[ c. 9      ]πάρχουσιν λοιπὸν [
   5  ] αλλοισ[ c. 9  σ]υντεταγμένα νῦν [
      ] . ομι . [ c. 10 ] ἡμᾶς ὑμῖν παρεῖναι[
      ]ζομε[ c. 10      ]τέρας συνμετρίας ὑμῖγ[
      ] δικαίων [ c. 10  ]ων βάλλοντες καταχωσαγ[τ
      ]ατε καὶ γ[c. 8  [[συ]υτρόφῳ κακείᾳ]] γένους ἐκ τῶν [
   10 ]τινω ὑλα[ c. 9  σ]υντρόφῳ κακείᾳ ἡ τῆς ἰδίας
         ]λομεγ[ . . ἀν]αγκάζοντες ἐπὶ τὸ τῆς ἀποδώσεως
      ]εισθαι ἡμεῖς γὰρ τοῖς μηδὲν ἐκδικηκόσιν οὐδεμίαν
      ] παυσάσθωσαν ἐπιβουλεύοντες τοῖς τῶν ἐπαρ-
```

14   ]θώσασι καὶ μήτε ..[...]των πλεονεξίαν αλογι-
         ]ωτο ...[..] ται̣[ς ἀνα]ξίαις (?) ὕβρεσιν τοὺς μη

Col. ii

16   (m. 2)   στην[
               η καὶ τ[.]ς [
               ἐπαρχιωτ[
               c. 3 cm. blank

4 ν in λοιπόν corr. from υ   9 κακίᾳ   10 κακίᾳ   11 ἀποδόσεως

(l. 2) '. . . blame . . . let him be armed against the . . . for the rest . . . other . . . what has been ordered now . . . us to be present with you . . . proportion for you . . . rights . . . throwing, having obscured . . . race from the . . . habitual evil, one's own . . . compelling at the . . . of the return . . . for we . . . nothing to those who have claimed nothing in court . . . let them stop plotting against the . . . and neither . . . greed, senseless . . . with unworthy insults . . . those who have not(hing) . . .'

1   Apparently not ἄρτι at the end.
3   This is the first instance of ὁπλίζω in a papyrus. The word occurs again in **144**(*a*).7.
5   E.g., ἄλλοις, ἄλλοι ϛ[, ἀλλ' οισ[.
10   η: ἤ or ἡ.
14   end: e.g., ἀλογί|[στως or ἃ λογί|[ζονται.
15   end: μή or a longer word beginning with those letters.

(*g*)   VIII 8ᶜ + 9ᶜ. 5.4 × 18.1 cm. Virtually nothing of these adjoining fragments is intelligible apart from a mention of tax collection in l. 6 and of men in 10 and 11. The top margin may be preserved, but the papyrus is so damaged that it is hard to tell.

                   ]   τα.[
           ]α.[.......]   καρ[
    ].ελ.[.....].....ομ[
         ].[...].[..]
5   ].[..]..[.]..[.] καὶ πρ̣οσ.[
        ].....[.]ης ἀπαιτ[
      ]..[.]....[.].ς ἐπιτα.[

]τ[.]υτω . [. . .]ο[. . .] .ρ[
]θησατε[. . .]αισπαν[
10   ]ε τῶ[ν ἀν]θρώπων [
]. . . . τ[ῶν ἀ]νθρώπω[ν
] . [. . .] . λογοι[.] . . [
]ρχι[. . .] . [.] . . . . . απ[
] . α . [
15   ]οι[

traces of 3 lines

5   πρὸς and another word, or some compound with προσ-, if the reading is correct.

6   Presumably a form of ἀπαιτέω or ἀπαίτησις.

7   A form of ἐπιτάσσω seems likely.

(*h-l*)   The following fragments are the largest and best preserved of a number of bits from **143**, none of which is well enough preserved to yield a single certain word.

(*h*)   VIII 10ᶜ. 1.3 × 2.4 cm.

⎯⎯⎯   ⎯⎯⎯
] . υρι[
]ατου[
]θειη[
]τοι[
⎯⎯⎯   ⎯⎯⎯

(*i*)   VIII 11ᶜ. 1.3 × 1.2 cm.

⎯⎯⎯   ⎯⎯⎯   ⎯⎯⎯   ⎯⎯⎯
]θουσ[
] . [
⎯⎯⎯   ⎯⎯⎯   ⎯⎯⎯   ⎯⎯⎯

(*j*)   VIII 12ᶜ. 0.8 × 1.1 cm. Text:]τω[.
(*k*)   VIII 15ᶜ. 1.8 × 2 cm.

⎯⎯⎯   ⎯⎯⎯   ⎯⎯⎯   ⎯⎯⎯
] . [
]κε . . [
] . α [.] . [
⎯⎯⎯   ⎯⎯⎯   ⎯⎯⎯   ⎯⎯⎯

(*l*)   VIII 19ᶜ. 3.3 × 6.7 cm.

—   —   —   —

```
              ] . [
         ]καρθαδ[
            ]μουγ[
           ] . σοι . [
  5      ] . ενατον . [
         ] . ιατιον[
         ]ετη . [
         ]γα[
```

—   —   —   —

5   The word division is presumably] . ἕνα τον . [or] . ἔνατον . [.

144

(*a*)   VIII 20ᶜ. 20.5 × 13 cm. Mentions of law courts and debts in this comparatively large but puzzling fragment may indicate a theme related to that handled in **143**(*f*). Part of the papyrus has been left adhering to the cover of the codex, as it could not have been removed without damaging the binding; cf. pp. 88-9. At the top a margin of ca. 2.5 cm. is preserved.

```
  →                    ] . ν λίθοις κ[εκ]ελευ[
                       ] . εθέντος τ . . . . [
                       ]φου μένειν ἐχο [
       ] . . . . . . [ . . . . . . ]μεν ἡμετέρα κρίσει κα[
  5    ]τος εστ . . [ . . . . δη]μοσίῳ . ραφ . . ς τὴν τε[
       ] . . . ατοσ . [ . . . . . ]θαι δύγοιτο καὶ ειπε[
       ] . . ἀγροίκων ὀφέλειαν επις ὁπλίζοι`γ΄το [
       ] μηδὲν ἀργὸν μηδεονενα[
       ] κοινῆς κρίσεως φανείη πε . . . [
  10      ] . . . γοτέραν λο . . . τεροισ . . . [
       ] . . λομένων πάντων, ὁ δὲ πέραν [
       ] . αμ᾽ ἀκέραστοι καὶ ἐνεργεῖς τὰ παγ[
       ] . . . . λεις αὐτῶν ἔτι καὶ ἀποβαλεῖν [
       ]τοσ . . . . . . . [ . . . . ] . ἔγνωκ . . [
  15   ] . νομένων δικαστηρίων ἀλλ᾽ ἐν μ[
       ]ρας ἀπονοίας κλοπαῖς ἐσχόλαζεν νυ . [
       ] . ειν πρέπον κατεφαίνετο συνορᾶν η α[
       ] . ιν ὅταν μάλιστα ὁ τῆς ἀδικείας α[
       ]μόνα ὅσαπερ ἐν ταῖς δημοσίαις κομιζ[
```

20]αι γένους καὶ ἀποσχήσεσθε τῶν δικασ[τηρίων
] γὰρ ὅτι τοῦ λοιποῦ αἱ μὲν συνήθεις ὑμ[ων
]ς ἤρτηται [. . .]οι γῦν σφόδρα δίκαιον κατ[
]οι δόσεσιν τῇ λίαν ἐν τῷ παρελθόντι χρόνῳ [
] . ἡμῖν ἐπαρχιώτας ἀποτετολμημένοις ἀνθρ[ωπ
25]ασις οὐ φανερὸν ῥύβδην ἀεὶ μεριζομέγους [
]κοι . . . . . . [

— — — — — — —

18 ἀδικίας

'. . . stones, ordered . . . remain . . . our judgement . . . public . . .
he should be able to and . . . debt of the country people . . . should
arm themselves . . . nothing slack or . . . common judgement may
appear . . . of all (that is owed?), but he (who goes?) beyond . . .
at once insatiable and energetic . . . and also discard their . . . courts,
but in . . . foolishness devoted himself to theft . . . it appeared
proper to consider . . . especially when the . . . of the injustice . . .
such as in the public . . . type, and stay away from courts . . . for
. . . that in the future your customary . . . has been hung upon . . .
now very just . . . contributions by the excessive . . . in past time
. . . for us, provincials, ventured, men . . . not clear, always distrib-
uted freely . . .'

4 Perhaps τῇ] μὲν ἡμετέρᾳ κρίσει, but μεν may be a verb ending.

5 δη]μοσίῳ τραφείς looks somewhat better than γραφῆς.

6 δύγοιτο: I have not found this form elsewhere, but it is formed
correctly from δύνομαι, a common by-form of δύναμαι (cf. Mandilaras,
The Verb § 96). The preceding -θαι is presumably the end of an
infinitive governed by this verb. At the end of the line εἰ πε[, εἶπε[ρ,
εἶπε[ν come into consideration.

7 ὁπλίζοι'γ'το: cf. ὁπιζ'έσ'θω in **143**(f).3. The preceding traces
are puzzling. Perhaps ἐπισοπλίζοιντο for ἐπεισοπλίζοιντο, but the
compound is not attested elsewhere.

8 μηδέν at the beginning of the line suggests μηδέ after ἀργόν,
but μὴ δέον is also a possible word division.

11 Since debts are mentioned in l. 5, ὀφ]ειλομένων πάντων is
tempting. In the translation above I have treated πέραν at the end of
the line as an adverb, but it may be the accusative of πέρας.

12 ἀκέραστοι is a more attractive reading than ἀπέραστοι.

16 It is not clear from the context whether the subject of

ἐσχόλαζεν is a particular individual or 'the evil-doer' in general. At the end of the line perhaps νῦν or νύχ[τωρ.

18 ὁ τῆς ἀδικείας ἀ[ρχηγός or the like would seem reasonable.

19 μόνα may be from μόνος, or it may be the end of a word such as ἡγε]μόνα. Then perhaps ὅσαπερ ἐν ταῖς δημοσίαις κομίζ[εται ἀποθήκαις. If that should be right, cf. in general 143(a).

24 ἀποτετολμημένοις: the perf. pas. part. of ἀποτολμάω is attested in both an active and a passive sense (LSJ s.v.); I cannot tell which is meant here. It may agree with ἡμῖν (or ἀνθρ[ώποις, if that is the supplement) or be used substantively.

25 ῥύβδην: here for the first time in a papyrus. It is not clear whether μεριζομένους should be understood as middle or as passive.

(b) VIII 21ᶜ. 1.1 × 1.5 cm. A few letters from the beginning of two lines. Text: κτ[²η η[.

(c) VIII 22ᶜ. 1.1 × 1.6 cm. Text:] . [²]τειν[³]τελε[.

(d) VIII 23ᶜ. 1.5 × 0.6 cm. Text:] . τα . [.

(e) VIII 24ᶜ. 1.7 × 0.5 cm. Text:] . οιπα[.

(f) VIII 25ᶜ. 3.7 × 6.5 cm.

$$
\begin{array}{ll}
 & \text{] . [. . . .]α} \\
 & \text{]ην προαν-} \\
 & \text{]ων ἐμπρο-} \\
 & \text{]ϊδόντες} \\
5 & \text{]νδεθέντων} \\
 & \text{]τωνετοσ . .} \\
 & \text{]ων ἐπιστρεφ[.]} \\
 & \text{ἄ]λλῳ τρόπῳ} \\
 & \text{]αις συλων} \\
10 & \text{]βολὴν αρα[}
\end{array}
$$

8 ο in τρόπῳ corr.

2 προαν-: or πρὸ αν-.

3 The words beginning with εμπρο- that have hitherto occurred in papyri are ἔμπροσθεν, ἐμπρόθεσμος, and ἐμπροθέσμως.

4 I.e., ἰδόντες or a compound thereof.

5 I.e., συ]νδεθέντων, ἐ]νδεθέντων,]ν δεθέντων,]ν δὲ θέντων.

9 συλων: συλῶν if from συλάω or σύλη, σύλων if from σῦλον. Of

these three words, only συλάω is attested in papyri published up to now.

(g)   VIII 26ᶜ. 3.8 × 2.5 cm.

---   ---   ---   ---   ---

```
              ]ο ὀφθαλμ[ . . ]
              ]ρου χρησίμου
              ] . εντα ἐπενο-
            ἐ]πειδὴ ἡ ἀπο
```

---   ---   ---   ---

2   χρησίμου: or perhaps χρῆσί μου, but the first person singular is not elsewhere used in the preserved portions of **143-4** and it is hard to think of a plausible context for χρῆσί μου in a document of this nature. I suppose χρὴ σίμου need not be considered.

4   ἀπὸ, ἀπ' ὀ-, or the beginning of a word continued in the next line.

(h)   VIII 27ᶜ. 5.5 × 15.8 cm. Not enough of this fragment remains for us to determine the nature of the malpractices of which it speaks. Exactors and praepositi are mentioned, but it is not clear whether they are regarded as malefactors or agents for restoring observance of the law.

---   ---   ---   ---   ---   ---

```
                        ] . ρ[
                     ]ν ταῖς τε κεφαλαϊ[
                     ]κον οὐκ ἂν οὔθ' ὁ . [
                     ] καὶ συμφέροντος [
        5            ]μεν ἰάματα προσ[
                     ]ατων τε ἐξακτόρ[ων
                     ]ᾀξίαν ἐστιν εναγησ[
                     ]ησελειν ὑπέχεσθαι[
                     ]ων ἀνομοτάτων τ[
        10           ] . [ . ] ὑμᾶς οὐ παυον[
                     ]ατήσαντες βου[
                     ]ας τούτων κατατ[
                     ]σιων τυγ'χάνουσ[
                     ]ν νόμων καὶ τη[
        15           ]ν ἀτοποτάτων [
                 ἐξάκτ]ωρ (?) ἢ πραιπόσιτος [
```

] ἡμετέρᾳ διορίσει ει[
]θεν πλημμέλημα[
]αι τοῖς παρὰ τοῖς ἡγεμ[ο
c. 3 cm. blank

2   The most obvious supplements at the end of the line are κεφαλαί[αις and κεφαλαι[ώδεσι, but there are other possibilities as well. The word is not necessarily dative: an expression such as ταῖς τε κεφαλαι[ωτῶν ἀδικίαις cannot be excluded.

5   The word ἴαμα appears to have occurred previously in papyri only in P. Laur. II 27v.2, if the reading is correct there.

6   Perhaps]α τῶν τε ἐξακτόρ[ων καὶ τῶν πραιποσίτων; cf. l. 16 and **143**(a).11-2 n.

7   The word at the end is probably ἐναγής, though a construction for ἕνα γῆς could perhaps also be found.

10   If the correct supplement is ὑμᾶς οὐ παύον[τας, the general sense will probably have been 'seeing that despite repeated warnings you do not cease from your misdeeds, we have determined to take the following measures'; but a different form of παύω with some quite other idea may have been written.

14   In this context νόμων in the sense of laws seems reasonably certain. Then perhaps τῆ[ς δίκης.

16   ἐξάκτ]ωρ (?): in view of the mention of exactors in l. 6 above and **143**(a).11 this supplement appears natural. Of thinkable alternatives, πράκτ]ωρ is probably excluded by the date: the latest reference to a practor in N. Lewis, *Inventory of Compulsory Services in Ptolemaic and Roman Egypt* (New Haven, 1968 = *ASP* 3) is A.D. 265. κουράτ]ωρ and κτήτ]ωρ, however, are perhaps just possible.

17   διορίσει: apparently not found elsewhere in papyri. *LSJ* s.v. cites the definitions 'separation' and 'division'; here 'pronouncement' or 'decision' seems to be called for.

18   πλημμέλημα rather than πλημμελήμα[τα on the assumption that the preceding]θεν is part of an adjective or participle modifying this word; but there are other possibilities, e.g. ὅ]θεν πλημμελήμα[τα γίνεται.

19   ἡγεμ[όσι, ἡγεμ[ονικοῖς, or a participle of ἡγεμονεύω. The idea may have been that the perpetrators of certain crimes are to be handed over to the agents of provincial governors, or that certain things are to be reported to them.

145. LETTER

VIII 28ᶜ + 29ᶜ   (a) 8 × 10.5 cm.   4th cent. A.D.
                        (b) 3.3 × 10.1 cm.

Two fragments of a private letter, too mutilated for translation.
Frag. (a) preserves part of the left margin; the relative position of
(b) can no longer be determined.

(a)

→   [.].[..].[...]πεληψ[
     ο[ὐ]κέτι παγεντα[
     αγ τῷ ἑνὶ ἢ τασ[
     τὰ νῦν τε ηὗρε[
5   [.]ων ... νον ιθ[
     [.]ου εξολατης[
     κατὰ ὄνομα κα.[
     [.]ε νῦ[ν] τὰ μηλ[
     [.].... ὅτι ἡ τ[
10   [.].....[.].ια σου [
     [.] ολλα..μην[

(b)

     ].ων..[
     ]απεληψ[
     ]αζομε[
15   ]ωθ μετα[
     ].ν ποιειτ[
     ].μασητη.[
     ]α οὔτε τη[
     ] νῦν τε[
20   ]ου σίτου [
     ] παρημελη[

Back:

→   ] πατρί μου Ηριγαμ[..]μ.[
     traces of 1 more line

7 κ in κα.[corr. from α   9 ἡ corr. from α

2   παγὲν τα[or παγέντα, if γ is correct.

4   At the end, ηὑρέ[θη or the like.

5   Perhaps τέχνον or τὸ λίνον before ιθ[.

6   εξολατης: if a single word, the term is new, and the derivation is not obvious. If ουεξολάτης should be written together, a connection with Latin *vexillum* might be considered, but the phonology is rather remote. Possibly the word division is ἐξ, ὁ Λάτης; for Lates as a personal name cf. P. Teb. IV 1139.5.

8   E.g., τὰ μῆλ[α, τὰ μηλ[οκοπικά, τὰ μὴ λ[, if η is in fact correct.

14   The letters preserved are suitable for a form of ἀσπάζομαι, but the following lines do not suggest greetings. A word such as λοιπ]αζόμε[να may therefore be more probable.

15   ]ωθ suggests an Egyptian name, such as the month Θώθ or Φαμενώθ.

22   No name beginning with Ηριγαμ- is recorded in the *NB* or *Onomasticon*, but the reading is very doubtful.

In addition to **143-5** and the Coptic texts **C15-9**, the cover of Codex VIII contained 83 bits of papyrus too fragmentary for transcription.

CODEX IX

Fifty small bits of papyrus written in hands of the late third or early fourth century A.D. Only seven are large enough to preserve a few words. The backs are blank unless otherwise noted.

146. IX 1ᶜ. 4.6 × 2.8. Written in a hand very similar to, and perhaps identical with, that of **44** and **45**. It may further be part of the same text as the following fragment. A top margin seems to be preserved.

→ φιλουμ . [

The Brussels MS reads φίλου μο[υ. On the plate the proper name Φιλούμε[νος also appears to be possible.

Back:

↓] . . . . [
   ] Φαῆρις α[

147. IX 2ᶜ. 5 × 2.8 cm. Possibly from the same document as **146**.

→]υιος[
   c. *1.8 cm. blank*
   ] . α[   ] . [

1 υἱός or part of a word or name such as Φλαο]ύιος.

Back:

↓ Φαῆρις ἀδελφό[ς
   c. *1.5 cm. blank*
   . [   ]κελ[

148. IX 3ᶜ. 4 × 2 cm. Account. The right margin seems to be preserved.

—   —   —   —

→   ] . αριω . . ιανος
        ] . κελει πόλεως
        ]   ὁμοῦ

—   —   —   —

2   It does not seem possible to read the name of any known city in this line. Possibly we are dealing with the collection of taxes, with a distinction made between sums owed by villagers and those owed by residents of a nome capital; cf. e.g. P. Oxy. XLIV 3169 introd.

149.   IX 4ᶜ. 5 × 2.8 cm. The top margin is preserved.

→   ] δι' ἡμῶν τω[
        ] . οτε . [

—   —   —   —

150.   IX 5ᶜ. 3.6 × 1.5 cm. Possibly in the same hand as **149**. The first word preserved, a form of μετρέω or a compound, suggests a connection with grain.

—   —   —   —

→   ]μετρησαν[
        ]ου . . . . [

—   —   —   —

151.   IX 6ᶜ. 3.6 × 2 cm. The text is written against the fibers, the other side being blank. Text: ↓] . . ξαυς . [, traces of 2 more lines.

152.   IX 7ᶜ. 4.4 × 1.8 cm. Evidently part of an account. Text:
→]β/ εκγ . [.

CODEX XI

153. LETTER

XI 1ᶜ   9.8 × 7 cm.   4th cent. A.D.

Little apart from the greeting of this fragmentary letter is still intelligible.

→   κυρίῳ μου ἀδελφῷ Π[
                Φ . . . ῆχις . [
        πρὸ μὲν πάντων [εὔχομαι τῷ Θεῷ]
        περὶ τῆς σῆς ὁλοκ[ληρίας
5   απημ . [.] . τηγ[
        ουκαλ . [. .]εμοι[
        ἐπεστιλ[
        . ησα . [
        —   —   —   —

Back:→   Φ . . . ῆ]χις Χηνοβωσχίτ(ης)

        9   Χηνοβοσκίτης

'To my lord brother P-, Ph . . . echis. First of all I pray to God concerning your well-being . . . (Back): (To P-), Ph . . . echis from Chenoboskia.'

2   The trace at the end of the line slightly favors π[λεῖστα or π[ολλὰ χαίρειν over simply χ[αίρειν or ἐ[ν Κ(υρί)ῳ χαίρειν.

3   εὔχομαι τῷ Θεῷ (or τῷ Κυρίῳ) is the minimal supplement. Longer formulations such as εὔχομαι τῷ ὑψίστῳ Θεῷ are also possible.

6   Two possible ways of understanding this line are οὐκ ἄλλ[ως] ἐμοί and οὐ καλῶ[ς] ἐμοί.

7   The traces would suit an aorist from ἐπιστέλλω spelled with iotacism after τ, but something like ἐπέστη λ[is also possible.

9   The word for 'an inhabitant of Chenoboskia' appears to be new.

INDEXES

I. EMPERORS AND REGNAL YEARS

Aurelian or Domitius Domitianus
] . ετίου   **62**.4 (?) *Cf.* II, A.D. 344.
Constantius II and Constans
οἱ δεσπόται ἡμῶν αἰώνιοι Αὔγουστοι   **65**.5-6 *See also* II, A.D. 346.
Uncertain
τοῦ αὐτοῦ ζ' . . . . ἔτους   **2**.3-4

II. CONSULS

ὑπατείας ᾿Αντωνίου Μαρκελλίνου καὶ Πετρωνίου Προβίνου τῶν λαμπροτάτων
(A.D. 341)   **63**.12-3
[ὑπατείας Φλαουίων Λεο]γτίου [καὶ Σαλλουστίου τῶν λαμπροτά]των (A.D. 344)
62.4-5 (? *See* p. 52, n. 3).
ὑπατείας τῶν δεσποτῶν ἡμῶν Κωνσταντίου Αὐγούστου τὸ δ καὶ Κώνσταντος
Αὐγούστου τὸ γ (A.D. 346)   **64**.1-3
[ὑπατείας Φλαυίου Φιλίππ]ου τοῦ λαμπροτάτου [ἐπάρχου τοῦ ἱεροῦ πραιτωρί]ου
καὶ Φλαυίου Σαλιᾶ [τοῦ λαμπροτάτου μαγίστρου ἱππέ]ων (A.D. 348) **65**.15-7

III. INDICTIONS

ς **26**.3,4 **64**.12 **82**.17n.

IV. MONTHS AND DAYS

'Αθὺρ κδ **63**.14 κε **64**.3   Παχών **62**.5n.
Θώθ **55**.4   Φαῶφ[ι] ι **65**.17

V. PERSONAL NAMES

b = brother of
d = daughter of
f = father of
gd = granddaughter of
gf = grandfather of
gs = grandson of

m = mother of
n = nephew of
s = son of
sis = sister of
u = uncle of

'Αβαρᾶς **66**.2
'Αβώ or 'Αβῶς **50**.4
'Αβῶς **54**.6
'Αγκάρας **85**.1n.
Αγω[**23**(b).4
'Αθανα[**82**.11
Αἴγυπτος **20**.2 (? perhaps a place
name)

Αχ[**23**(d).5
Αλ[f Kerapoubeus **45**(b).5
'Αλεύς f Dioskoros and Philon, gf
Arrios **45**(b).10
Απ- **23**(d).7
'Απο- **73**.2
'Απολ- **33**.1
'Απολλ(ω) s Hierakapollon **22**(i). 14

Ἀπολλωνίδης 22(i).15
Ἀπολλώνιος supervisor 22(g).8
Ἀππιανός 68.4
Ἀπσηνᾶς f Pachoumis 85.2
Ἀρακλῦς 69.24,26
Ἀρμογῖς f Aur. Comes 64.4
Ἁρποκρατίων 68.2, 23
Ἄρριος s Philon, gs Aleus, n Dioskoros 45(b).12
Ἀτρῆς 51.10
Ἀτρῆς s Ep- 51.9
Ἁ[ὺ]ρ[95.1
Αὐρηλι- 90.1
Αὐρηλία(?) Θεοδώρα 65.7
Αὐρήλιος NN 62.8
Αὐρήλιος Κόμης s Harmogis 64.4
Αὐρήλιος Μέλας 65.2
Αὐρήλιος Πτολεμαῖος s Pachoumis, former magistrate 64.5
Αὐρήλιος Στατίλλιος s Deuteros, former magistrate 63.17
Αὐρήλιος Ψενετῦμις 63.14,20
Ἀφροδίσιος 69.[1],5,7
Ἀχ[46.9
Ἀχιλλεύς 29.9

Βῆκις 82.14
Βησαρίων 75.3 77.10
Βοάις 70.17,19
Βουκόλος s Sto- 58.1 (? Cf. n.).

Γεώργιος 49.1

Δ. . .ς s Patra- 45(a).1
Δελχός or Δελχοῦς f Phaeris, gf Dioskoros 44(a).5
Δεύτερος f Aur. Statillius 63.17
Δημητ[f Horion 25.2
Δίδυμος 27.5
Δίδυμος f Sarapion 26.3
Δῖος 101v.n.
Διοσ(—) 1.1n.
Διοσκο- f Zenon 45(b).17
Διόσκορος 29.10 44(b).3
Διόσκορος s Aleus, b Philon, u Arrios 45(b).10
Διόσκορος s Chales, gs Eleus, b Phaminia(?) 44(b).6
Διόσκορος s Herakles 44(a).8

Διόσκορος s Opeionis, b Ma- 45(b).15
Διόσκορος s Phaeris, gs Delchos 44(a).5
Διόσκορος s Sennis, gs Ser- 45(a).3
Δόρκων presbyter 71.20

Ε. .βαι[54.4
Ἐλεύς f Chales, gf Phaminia(?) and Dioskoros 44(b).5
Εμποσ(—) 49.2
Επ[f Hatres 51.9
Επ. .ε[54.3
Ἐπαίνετος 54.3n.
Ἐπίμαχος 22(c).4,9n.
Ἐπω[51.1
Ἐπώνυχος 45(b).4 49.4 82.3
Ἑρμεῖνος, NN also called, s Eudaimon 2.6
Ἔρως f Philon, gf NN 45(a).8
Εὐδαίμων 23(a).3n.
Εὐδαίμων f NN also called Hermeinos 2.6
Εὐδαίμων f NN (Pimelis ?) also called Kopreas 2.9
Εὐναιτ- 4.2
Εὐσεβείων 23(d).9

Ζαχέος presbyter 77.16 78.2,15
Ζήνων s Diosko- 45(b).17

Η.ου[45(b).16
Ηδεμυδρα 1.6
Ἧλις s Plous 44(a).10
Ηρ[22(i).16
Ἡράκλειος 78.7
Ἡράκλειος shepherd 45(a).4
Ἡρακλῆς 43.2
Ἡρακλῆς f Dioskoros 44(a).8
Ηριγαμ[145.22
Θερ[29.8 42v
Θεοδώρα see Αὐρηλία Θ.
Θεότιμος 22(i).16
Θέων 22(i).1

Ι[22(h).9
Ἰβίων 57r (?)
Ἱερακαπόλλων f Apollo( ) 22(i).14
Ἱερακίων 22(i).9

Πεκύσιος 66.22
Πεκῦσις 1.3
Πεκῦσις s M- 52.1
Πεκῦσις s Sikles, f -on 44(e).2
Πενδ.εύς f Phaeris 44(a).6
Πενθ.[47.4
Πε. .τῖνος 26.2
Πετεῆσις 74.2
Πέτρος 68.3
Πεχενεφγῖβις, presbyter 77.17
Πι[f Lolous 51.4
Πικῶς 54.5
Πιμέλις ὁ καὶ Κοπρεᾶς s Eudaimon 2.9n.,10
Πλελοῦς 45(b).2(?)
Πλη[87.1
Πλῆνις 22(c).5
Πλοῦς f Elis 44(a).10
Πόλλων s Cornelius 23(d).8n.
Πόλλων s Ktesias 23(d).5n.
Πρήτ 75.8
Προτερία (Προτηρία) 72.2(?),15(?)
Πσᾶς or Πσάτος, monch 72.1,16
Πτολεμαῖος see Αὐρήλιος Π.

Σ. 46.5
Σανεῖς 82.4
Σανσνῶς 69.2 (same as following ?)
Σανσνῶς monch, presbyter 72.1,16 78.[1],15 and probably 68.1,22 73.2(?) 75.2 76.1 77.16
Σανσνῶς shepherd 69.17,20
Σανσνῶς s Chollos 44(b).7
Σανσνῶς s M- 44(d).8
Σα]ραπίων 23(b).8
Σαραπίων s Didymos 26.3
Σαχαρίας 82.4
Σεναμοῦνις m Panameus 44(a).3
Σενεβοῦνις 52.4
Σενθα[47.3
Σέννις s Ser-, f Dioskoros 45(a).3
Σενφ.[47.6
Σενφαῆρις 52.3
Σεουῆρος, supervisor 27.2
Σερ.[f Sennis, gf Dioskoros 45(a).3
Σ]εράπις(?) 57.6n.
Σέρβις f Paḳyras 44(a).4
Σι. .[f Phaeris 61.3

Σιεν[82.16
Σικλῆς f Pekysis, gf -on 44(e).2
Σιλ[44(c).1
Σιλβα[82.12
Σιλβανός 23(b).6 87.1
Σιλβανός s Kalei- 45(b).9
Σιλεμ[44(c).2
Σοισοιεῖς 82.5
Σοκῆς 48v.1
Σογ.[44(c).3
Στατίλλιος See Αὐρήλιος Σ.
Στο.[f Boukolos (? cf. n.) 58.1
Σῦρος 23(d).3 76.4 (? perhaps place name)
Σῦρος f Psais 22(i).10

Ταπῆς 44(b).3n.
Τεκῶσις 57.4n.
Τεῷς 50.2
Τιβερῖνος 23(b).3
Τούρβων s Phaeris 44(a).9
Τριάδελφος f -on 44(e).1
Τριφ[4.6
Τριφρονῶς(?) 2.8

Φ[37.2
Φ[f Moros 49.3
Φα.[64.13
Φαῆρ(ις) 51.5
Φαῆρις 44(d).1,5 54.10 146v.2 147v.1
Φαῆρις s Delchos, f Dioskoros 44(a).5
Φαῆρις s Kel- 44(d).6
Φαῆρις s Kelemmares 45(a).6
Φαῆρις s Midas 44(a).7
Φαῆρις s P- 44(a).11
Φαῆρις s P-, b Paulos and Makarios 45(b).7
Φαῆρις s Pend.eus 44(a).6
Φαῆρις s Phamies 45(a).5
Φαῆρις s Si- 61.3
Φαῆρις f Tourbon 44(a).9
Φαησ[51.3
Φαμιῆς 45(a).5
Φαμινία(?) d Chales, gd Eleus, sis Dioskoros 44(b).5n.
Φατρῆς 44(a).2
Φε. .[29.7 (? perhaps place name)

8

Φενψετύμης **70**.1,22
Φ.. ῆχις **153**.2,9
Φιλούμενος **146**r.n.
Φιλούμενος f Horos **48**v.2
Φίλων s Aleus, f Arrios, b Dioskoros **45**(b).11
Φίλων s Eros, f NN **45**(a).8

Χαλῆς s Eleus, f Phaminia(?) and Dioskoros **44**(b).5
Χενοφρῆς **70**.[2],22
Χολλῶς f Sansnos and others **44**(b).7

Ψάις s Syros **22**(i).10
Ψαρφει.[**47**.2
Ψεκῆς f Psekes **85**.3
Ψεκῆς s Psekes **85**.3
Ψενε[**54**.9
Ψενε.[**54**.7
Ψενετῦμις See Αὐρήλιος Ψ.
Ψεντεκῶσις **52**.5

Ω[**29**.6
'Ωρ[**29**.2
'Ωρίων **71**.20 **82**.7
'Ωρίων s Demeṭ- **25**.2
'Ωρίων s Kallos **45**(a).7
ʹΩρος s Philoumenos **48**v.2
Ωσι.[**128**.2

Doubtful (Selected)

]αβῦγχις s Kentis **44**(e).3
α]πόλλωνος (gen.) s Cornelius **23**(d).8n.
ἀ]πόλλωνος (gen.) s Ktesias **23**(d).5n.
]άριος presbyter **71**.20
]ατενοῦς **30**.1
]εράπις **57**.6
].ιανός s Pe .. tinos **26**.2
].πίωνος (gen.?) s Pasis **26**.4
]ωνι ἐνάρχῳ προέδρῳ **65**.1

VI. GEOGRAPHY

Αἴγυπτος **20**.2 (? perhaps a personal name)
'Ανταιοπολίτης **22**(i).11
'Απόλλωνος κάτω **22**(i).8
Δι.[.].. . **23**(c).3
Διοσπολ- **101**v
Διὸς πόλις **1**.1n.,4 **101**v.n. *Cf.* **23**(c).3n.
Διοσπολίτης νομός **64**.5
'Ερμοπολίτης **22**(h).3
Θηβαίς **23**(a).6n.
 Θ. ἄνω **22**(c).3 **23**(c).15
 Θ. κάτω **22**(c).6,(h).1 **23**(c).14
'Ιβιών **57**r (?)

Κάριος **3**.9n. **66**.8
Κουσσίτης **22**(h).8
Πανοπολίτης **22**(i).13
Σύρου **76**.4 (? perhaps a personal name)
Τεντυριτῶν πόλις **64**.6
Τεχθύ (Diopolite village) **64**.4
'Υψηλίτης **22**(i).5
Φε..[**29**.7 (? perhaps a personal name)
Χηνοβόσκια **1**.4 **31**.3
Χηνοβοσκίτης **153**.9 (pap. χηνοβω-σχι[τ])
]οπολείτου **23**(b).2

VII. OFFICIAL AND MILITARY TERMS AND TITLES

ἄρξας **63**.18 **64**.6
διεπιτροπή **22**(h).1
ἐξάκτωρ **143**(a).11 **144**(h).6,16(?)
ἔπαρχος τοῦ ἱεροῦ πραιτωρίου see II (A.D. 348).
ἐπιμελητής **22**(c).4n.,(g).8 **26**.2 **27**.2,3,5,6
ἐπιστράτηγος **53**.2n. **56**.4n.
ἐπιτροπή **22**(c).3,[6]

ἡγεμο[**144**(h).19
ἱππεύς see μάγιστρος.
μάγιστρος ἱππέων see II (A.D. 348).
πραιπόσιτος **143**(a).11n. **144**(h).16
πρόεδρος **65**.1
προεστώς **1**.7
στρατηγός **53**.2n. **56**.4n.
τείρων **66**.15
ὑπατεία see II.

VIII. RELIGION

IX. CURRENCY AND MEASURES

A. Currency

B. Measures

X. TAXES

XI. GENERAL INDEX OF WORDS

ἴαμα **144**(h).5
ἰατρός **6**.1
ἰβιών *see* VI.
ἴδιος **69**.23 **143**(f).10
ἰδού **71**.9
ἱερός *see* VII, s.v. ἔπαρχος.
ἵνα **70**.9 **72**.12 **77**.8,10 **78**.[5]
ἰνδικτίων *see* III.
ἱππεύς *see* VII, s.v. μάγιστρος.
ἱστορέω **6**.2n.
ἱστορία **6**.2n.
ἰσχύω **3**.7

καθώς **69**.3
καιρός **64**.10 **68**.7
κακία **143**(f).9-10
καλός **153**.6n.
καλῶς **2**.11 **153**.6n.
Κάριος *see* VI.
κατά (with gen.) **143**(f).3
  (with acc.) **1**.11 **68**.9 **70**.4 **71**.15
  77.12 **79**.11,15
  143(a).16n. **145**.7
καταλαμβάνω **66**.9,12
κατασπορά **64**.11
καταφαίνω **144**(a).17
καταχώννυμι **143**(f).8
κάτω *see* VI, s.v. 'Απόλλωνος and
  Θηβαίς.
κείρω **66**.7,18
κελεύω **144**(a).1
κεφαλαι- **144**(h).2
κίνδυνος **65**.11 **143**(b).15
κινέω **143**(e).4
κληρονόμος **51**.1,3(?)
κλοπή **144**(a).16
κοινῇ **1**.9
κοινός **144**(a).9
κόκκος **64**.13
κομίζω **144**(a).19
κριθή **18**.1 **19**(b).4 **46**.3 **50**.3,7,10,16
  51.8
κρίσις **143**(b).5 **144**(a).4,9
κτῆνος **67**.9 **69**.13 **72**.6
κυβερνήτης **25**.1(?), 3n.
κύριος (lord) **4**.1 **66**.1 **74**.1 **75**.1
  81.14 **153**.1
  (the Lord) *see* VIII.

(adj.) **2**.10 **62**.[3] **65**.[12]
κώμη **1**.5,7 **64**.4

λαμβάνω **66**.16,20,23,25
λαμπρότατος **62**.5n. **63**.13 **65**.15,
  [17]
λαχανᾶς **44**(b).2n.
λάχανον **70**.6
λέβης **3**.28,[29]
λέγω **4**.7 *Cf.* εἶπον, ἐρῶ.
λευκός **3**.10
λῆμμα **25**.2n. **29**.3,7
λίαν **144**(a).23
λίθος **144**(a).1
λογίζομαι **143**(f).14n.
λόγος **143**(a).16n., (b).8, (g).12(?)
λοιπ- **143**(a).4
λοιπάζω **69**.20
λοιπός
  λοιπόν **143**(f).4
  τοῦ λοιποῦ **144**(a).21

μάγιστρος ἱππέων *see* VII.
μάλα **71**.9
μάλιστα **144**(a).18
μανθάνω **69**.24 **71**.11,17
μάτιον *see* IX, B.
μαφόρτιον **2**.9n.
μέμψις **143**(f).2
μέν **143**(b).7 **153**.3
μένω **144**(a).3
μερίζω **144**(a).25
μετά (with gen.) **63**.2 **68**.17
μετα[**74**.27
μετακομίζω **67**.8
με[τ]ρ[**55**.4
(—)μετρέω **150**.1
μέτρον *see* IX, B.
μέχρι **63**.[6] **64**.[16]
μή **1**.14 **2**.4 **63**.[4],19 **65**.[10] **66**.10
  67.11 **70**.10 **71**.17 **77**.9 **81**.9
  144(a).8n.
μηδέ **144**(a).8n.
μηδείς **143**(f).12 **144**(a).8
μήν (month) **28**.1n.
μήτε **143**(f).14
μήτηρ **65**.[8]
μνᾶ *see* IX, B.

PART TWO

THE COPTIC PAPYRI

BY

J. W. B. BARNS† AND GERALD M. BROWNE

CONTENTS

TABLE OF PAPYRI

PREFACE

In preparing this edition of Coptic papyri from the covers of the Nag Hammadi Codices, I have had the good fortune to have at my disposal the preliminary transcripts and notes of the late Professor J. W. B. Barns. What he accomplished before his untimely death greatly aided my work, and the quality of the present edition is significantly enhanced by his contribution. I have examined the originals twice in the Coptic Museum, Old Cairo, once in the summer of 1974, and again in December 1976. The first visit to Cairo was funded by the Smithsonian Institution through the sponsorship of the American Research Center in Egypt, the second by the University of Illinois at Urbana-Champaign; to each organization I am grateful for the financial support which made the completion of this edition possible.

Gerald M. Browne
Urbana, Illinois
26 February 1979

CODEX I

1 COPTIC FRAGMENT

Inv. I 13ᶜ: 2 × 2 cm.

The only piece in codex I which is in Coptic is a tiny fragment of which only two letters can be read; the first seems clearly a ⲱ, while the second may be an ⲁ. The verso is blank.

$$\longrightarrow \quad \begin{array}{c} - - - - - - - \\ ]\,.\,.\,[\\ ]\omega\,.\,\text{ⲁ}\,.\,[\\ - - - - - - - \end{array}$$

CODEX VII

2 GENESIS 32.5-21 AND 42.27-30, 35-38

Inv. VII 89ᶜ: 11 × 8.5 cm.; 90ᶜ: 11 × 16.5 cm.; 91ᶜ: 6 × 10 cm.; 92ᶜ: 0.75 × 0.25 cm.; 93ᶜ: 1.00 × 0.60 cm.

With the exception of the exiguous fragments 92ᶜ and 93ᶜ, this text was first published by R. Kasser, "Fragments du livre biblique de la Genèse cachés dans la reliure d'un codex gnostique," *Le Muséon* 85 (1972) 65-89; to this article the reader is referred for a detailed treatment of the problems involved. The present re-edition provides a revised transcription, equipped with translation, and the commentary indicates the differences between the new transcript and Kasser's. Throughout we have substituted the more conventional dots for Kasser's half brackets (⌞ and ⌟); these signs he uses for letters which are damaged but certain as well as for those whose reading is in doubt. In the re-edition we employ a dot only where the letter cannot be read with certainty, and we usually do not record the reading of Kasser's text if it differs from ours only in the case of dotted letters.

Kasser regarded the two folios which the text comprises as parts of a double leaf, of which 89ᶜ and 90ᶜ came from one half and 91ᶜ from the other. On the basis of this assumption he proceeded to give a reconstruction of the entire codex, and he believed that the first folio bore the page numbers 31-32 and the second 69-70 (see pp. 72-74 for his discussion). Only horizontal fiber alignment between the two folios would demonstrate the correctness of Kasser's assumption, and despite repeated autoptic examination of the text in Cairo, we have been unable to detect any indication of such alignment. Consequently the hypothesis that the text comes from a double leaf is hardly possible, and in the re-edition we have preferred to adopt a neutral position and have labeled the two folios as X and Y respectively.

We have had no success in placing the tiny fragments 92ᶜ and 93ᶜ. They cannot fit in with the text lost in folio X, and they may have come from the lost portion of Y.

The text should probably be assigned to the late third or early fourth century of our era; see Kasser, 76.

In the commentary, we use the following abbreviations: K = Kasser; Ceugney = C. Ceugney, "Quelques fragments coptes-thébains inédits de la Bibliothèque Nationale," *Recueil de travaux relatifs à la philologie et à l'archéologie égyptiennes et assyriennes* 2 (1880) 94-105; Ciasca = A. Ciasca, *Sacrorum Bibliorum fragmenta copto-sahidica Musei Borgiani* 1 (Rome 1885).

FOLIO X

Recto

↓ 89ᶜ

ⲁϥϩⲱⲛ ⲉⲧⲟ[ⲟ]ⲧⲟⲩ ⲉϥϫⲱ ⲙ̅ⲙⲟⲥ·   32.5
ϫⲉ ⲧⲁⲉⲓ ⲧⲉ ⲑⲉ ⲉⲧⲉⲧⲛⲁϫⲟⲟⲥ ⲙ̅
ⲡⲁϫⲟⲉⲓⲥ ⲏⲥⲁⲩ ϫⲉ ⲧⲁⲉⲓ ⲧⲉ ⲑⲉ ⲉ
ⲧϥ̅ϫⲱ ⲙ̅ⲙⲟⲥ· ϫⲉ ⲡⲉⲕϩⲙ̅ϩⲁⲗ ⲓ̈
5 ⲁⲕⲱⲃ ϫⲉ ⲁⲉⲓⲟⲩⲱϩ ⲙⲛ̅ ⲗⲁⲃⲁⲛ   6
ⲁⲉⲓⲱⲥⲕ̅· ϣⲁ ϩⲣⲁⲓ̈ ⲉⲡⲟⲟⲩ ⲁⲩϣⲱ
ⲡ[ⲉ] ⲛⲁⲓ̈ ⲛ̅ϭⲓ ϩⲉⲛⲉⲥⲟⲟⲩ ⲙⲛ̅ ϩⲉⲛ
[ⲉϩⲟ]ⲟⲩ ϩⲛ̅ϩⲙ̅ϩⲁⲗ ⲛ̅ϩⲟⲟⲩⲧ ⲙⲛ̅
[ϩⲉⲛ]ϩⲙ̅ϩⲁⲗ ⲛ̅ⲥϩⲓⲙⲉ· ⲁⲉⲓⲧⲛ̅
10 [ⲛⲟⲟ]ⲩ ⲉϫⲉⲓ ⲡⲟⲩⲱ ⲛ̅ⲏⲥⲁⲩ ⲡⲁϫⲟ
[ⲉⲓ]ⲥ· ϫⲉ ⲉⲣⲉ ⲡⲉⲕϩⲙ̅ϩⲁⲗ· ϩⲉ ⲉⲩ
[ϩ]ⲙⲟⲧ ⲙ̅ⲡⲉⲕⲙ̅ⲧⲟ ⲉⲃⲟⲗ· [[.]] ⲁⲩⲕⲟ   7
[ⲧⲟ]ⲩ ⲛ̅ϭⲓ ⲛ̅ϥⲁⲓϣⲓⲛⲉ ϣⲁ ⲓ̈ⲁⲕⲱⲃ
[ⲉⲩϫⲱ] ⲙ̅[ⲙⲟⲥ ϫⲉ ⲁⲛⲃⲱⲕ ϣⲁ] ⲡ[ⲉⲕ]
15 [ⲥⲟⲛ ⲏⲥⲁⲩ ⲁⲩⲱ ⲉⲓⲥ ϩⲏⲏⲧⲉ ⲛⲧⲟϥ]
[ϥⲛⲏⲩ ⲉⲧⲱⲙⲧ ⲉⲣⲟⲕ ⲙⲛ ϥⲧⲉⲩ]
[ϣⲉ ⲛⲣⲱⲙⲉ ⲛⲙⲙⲁϥ ⲁ ⲓⲁⲕⲱⲃ ⲇⲉ]   8
90ᶜ   [ⲣ] ϩⲟⲧⲉ ⲉⲙⲁⲧⲉ ⲁⲩⲱ ⲁϥⲣ ϩⲃ[ⲁ]
ⲁϥⲡⲱ̅ϣ ⲙ̅ⲡⲗⲁⲟⲥ ⲉⲧⲛ̅ⲙⲙⲁϥ
20 ⲙⲛ̅ ⲛⲉϩⲟⲟⲩ ⲙⲛ̅ ⲛⲉⲥⲟⲟⲩ ⲉⲡ
[ⲡ]ⲁⲣⲉⲙⲃⲟⲗⲏ ⲥⲛ̅ⲧⲉ· ⲁⲩⲱ ⲡⲉ   9
ϫⲁϥ ⲛ̅ϭⲓ ⲓ̈ⲁⲕⲱⲃ· ⲉⲣϣⲁ ⲏⲥⲁⲩ
ⲉⲓ· ⲉⲧϣⲟⲣⲡ̅· ⲙ̅ⲡⲁⲣⲉⲙⲃⲟⲗⲏ ⲛϥ̅
[ϭ]ⲉⲭϭⲱϭⲧ̅ ⲧⲙⲉϩⲥⲛ̅ⲧⲉ ⲛⲁ̅ϣⲱ
25 ⲡⲉ ⲉⲥⲟⲩⲟⲟϫ· ⲡⲉϫⲁϥ ⲇⲉ ⲛ̅ϭⲓ ⲓ̈   10
ⲁⲕⲱⲃ· ϫⲉ ⲡⲛⲟⲩⲧⲉ ⲙ̅ⲡⲁⲉⲓⲱⲧ
ⲁⲃⲣⲁϩⲁⲙ· ⲁⲩⲱ ⲡⲛⲟⲩⲧⲉ ⲙ̅ⲡⲁ
ⲉⲓⲱⲧ ⲓ̈ⲥⲁⲁⲕ· ⲡϫⲟⲉⲓⲥ ⲡⲛⲟⲩⲧⲉ
ⲡⲉⲛⲧⲁϥϫⲟⲟⲥ ⲛⲁⲓ̈· ϫⲉ ⲃⲱⲕ ⲉϩ
30 ⲣⲁⲓ̈ ⲉⲡⲕⲁϩ· ⲉⲛⲧⲁⲩϫⲡⲟⲕ ϩⲣⲁⲓ̈

9

ⲛ̄ϩⲏⲧϥ̄ ⲧⲁⲣ̄ ⲡⲉⲧⲛⲁⲛⲟⲩϥ ⲛⲁⲕ
ⲁⲣⲓ ⲛⲁϣⲧⲉ· ⲛⲁⲓ̈ ⲉⲃⲟⲗ ϩⲛ̄ ⲇⲓⲕⲁⲓ   11
ⲟⲥⲩⲛⲏ ⲛⲓⲙ· ⲁⲩⲱ ⲉⲃⲟⲗ ϩⲙ̄ ⲙⲉ
ⲛⲓⲙ· ⲉⲛⲧⲁⲕⲁⲁⲩ ⲙⲛ̄ ⲡⲉⲕϩⲙ̄
35   ϩⲁⲗ· ϩⲣⲁⲓ̈ ⲅⲁⲣ ϩⲙ̄ ⲡⲁϭⲉⲣⲱⲃ
ⲁⲓ̈ϫⲓⲟⲟⲣ ⲙ̄ⲡⲓ̈ⲟⲣⲇⲁⲛⲏⲥ ϯⲛⲟⲩ
ⲇⲉ ⲁⲉⲓⲣ̄ ⲡⲁⲣⲉⲙⲃⲟⲗⲏ ⲥⲛ̄ⲧⲉ
ⲙⲁⲧⲟⲩⲭⲟⲉⲓ ⲉⲃⲟⲗ ϩⲛ̄ ⲧϭⲓⲝ·   12
ⲛ̄ⲏⲥⲁⲩ ⲡⲁⲥⲟⲛ. ϫⲉ ϯⲣ̄ ϩⲟⲧⲉ ⲁ̄
40   ⲛⲟⲕ ϩⲏⲧϥ̄ ⲙⲏⲡⲟⲧⲉ ⲛϥ̄ⲉⲓ

Verso

→ 89ᶜ   ⲉⲣⲱϩⲧ̄ ⲙⲙⲟⲉⲓ [ⲁⲩ]ⲱ ⲙ̣ⲙⲁⲁⲩ [ⲉϩ]
ⲣⲁⲓ̈ ⲉϫⲛ̄ ⲛⲉⲩϣⲏⲣⲉ ⲛ̄ⲧⲟⲕ ⲇⲉ   13
ⲁⲕϫⲟⲟⲥ ⲛⲁⲓ̈ ϫⲉ ϯⲛⲁⲣ̄ ⲡⲉⲧⲛⲁ
ⲛⲟⲩϥ ⲛⲁⲕ· ⲁⲩⲱ ϯⲛⲁⲕⲱ ⲙ̄ⲡⲉⲕ
5   ⲥⲡⲉⲣⲙⲁ· ⲛ̄ⲑⲉ ⲙ̄ⲡϣⲱ ⲛ̄ⲧⲉⲑⲁ
ⲗⲁⲥⲥⲁ· ⲡⲁⲉⲓ ⲉⲧⲉ ⲙⲉⲩⲟⲡϥ̄ ϩⲙ̄
ⲡⲉϥⲁϣⲁⲉⲓ· ⲁϥⲛ̄ⲕⲟⲧⲕ̄ ⲙ̄[ⲡⲙⲁ]   14
ⲉⲧⲙ̄ⲙⲁⲩ ⲛ̄ⲧⲉⲩϣⲏ ⲉⲧⲙ̄ⲙ[ⲁⲩ]
ⲁϥϫⲓ ⲛ̄ϩⲉⲛⲇⲱⲣⲟⲛ ⲉⲃⲟⲗ ϩ[ⲛ]
10   ⲛⲉ[[ⲧ]]ⲛⲧⲁϥⲉⲛⲧⲟⲩ ⲁϥϫⲟⲟⲩ[ⲥⲟⲩ]
ⲛ̄ⲏⲥⲁⲩ ⲡⲉϥⲥⲟⲛ· ϣⲏⲧ ⲛ̄ⲃⲁ   15
ⲁⲙⲡⲉ· ϫⲟⲩⲱⲧ ⲛ̄ϭⲉⲓⲉ· ϣⲏⲧ ⲛ̄
ⲉⲥⲟⲟⲩ· ϫⲟⲩⲱⲧ· ⲛ̄ⲟⲉⲓⲗⲉ· ⲙⲁ   16
ⲁⲃ ⲛ̄[ϭ]ⲁ̣ⲙⲟⲩⲗ ⲉ[ⲩⲧⲥ]ⲛ̄[ⲕⲟ] ⲛ̄
15   [ⲛⲉⲩϣⲏⲣⲉ ϩⲙⲉ ⲛⲉϩⲉ ⲙⲏⲧ]
[ⲙⲙⲁⲥⲉ ϫⲟⲩⲱⲧ ⲛⲉⲓⲱ ⲙⲏⲧ]
[ⲛⲥⲏϭ ⲁϥⲧⲁⲁⲩ ⲉⲃⲟⲗ ϩⲓⲧⲛ]   17
90ᶜ   ⲛ[ϭ]ⲓ̣[ϫ] ⲛ̄ⲛⲉ[ϥ]ϩⲙ̄ϩⲁⲗ· ⲡⲟϩⲉ
ⲡⲟϩⲉ ⲙⲁⲩⲁⲁϥ· ⲡⲉϫⲁϥ ⲇⲉ
20   ⲛ̄ⲛⲉϥϩⲙ̄ϩⲁⲗ· ϫⲉ ⲙⲟϣⲉ ϩⲁ
ⲧⲁϩⲏ· ⲛ̄ⲧⲉⲧⲛ̄ⲉⲓⲣⲉ ⲛ̄ⲟⲩ
ⲡⲱⲣⲝ· ⲛ̄ⲧⲙⲏⲧⲉ ⲛ̄ⲛⲟⲩⲟϩⲉ
ⲉⲩⲟϩⲉ· ⲁϥϩⲱⲛ ⲉⲧⲟⲟⲧϥ̄ ⲙ̄ⲡ   18
ϣⲟⲣⲡ̄ ⲉϥϫⲱ ⲙ̄ⲙⲟⲥ· ϫⲉ ⲉⲣ
25   ϣⲁⲛ ⲏⲥⲁⲩ ⲡⲁⲥⲟⲛ ⲧⲱⲙⲧ̄·
ⲉⲣⲟⲕ· ⲛϥ̄ϫⲛⲟⲩⲕ ⲉϥϫⲱ ⲙ̄ⲙ[ⲟⲥ]
ϫⲉ ⲉⲕⲏⲡ ⲉⲛⲓⲙ· ⲁⲩⲱ ⲉⲕⲛⲁ
ⲉⲧⲱⲛ· ⲁⲩⲱ ⲛⲁ ⲛⲓⲙ ⲛⲉ ⲛⲁⲉⲓ

ⲉⲧⲙⲟϣⲉ ϩⲁ ⲧⲉⲕϩⲏ· ⲉⲕⲉⲭⲟ   19
30 [ⲟ]ⲥ ⲛⲁϥ ϫⲉ ⲛⲁ ⲡⲉⲕϩⲙ̄ϩⲁⲗ ⲓ̈
ⲓ̈ⲁ[ⲕ]ⲱ̣[ⲃ ⲛⲉ] ⲛ̄[ⲁ]ⲱⲣⲟⲛ ⲛⲉⲛⲧⲁϥ
ⲧⲛ̄ⲛⲟⲟⲩⲥⲉ ⲙ̄ⲡⲉϥϫⲟⲉⲓⲥ ⲛ̄ⲥⲁⲩ
ⲁⲩⲱ ⲉⲓⲥ ϩⲏⲏⲡⲉ· ϩⲱⲱϥ ϥⲟⲩ
ⲏϩ ⲛ̄ⲥⲱⲛ· ⲁϥϩⲱⲛ ⲉⲧⲟⲟⲧ̄ϥ   20
35 ⲙ̄ⲡϣⲟⲣⲡ· ⲙⲛ̄ ⲡⲙⲉⲩⲥⲛ̄ⲁⲩ
ⲁⲩⲱ ⲡⲙⲉϩϣⲟⲙⲧ̄ ⲙⲛ̄ ⲟⲩⲟⲛ
ⲛ[ⲓ]ⲙ ⲉⲧⲟⲩⲏϩ· ⲛ̄ⲥⲁ ⲛ̄ⲧⲃ̄ⲛⲟⲟⲩ[ⲉ]
ⲉ[ϥ]ϫⲱ ⲙⲙⲟⲥ ϫⲉ ⲕ̣ⲁ̣ⲧ̣ⲁ̣ ⲡⲉⲓϣ[ⲁ]
ϫ̣ⲉ̣ ⲉ̣ⲧⲉⲧⲛ̄ⲉϣⲁϫⲉ ⲙⲛ ⲛⲥⲁⲩ
40 ϩⲙ̄ ⲡ[ⲧ]ⲣⲉⲧⲉⲧⲛ̄ⲧⲱⲙⲧ ⲉⲣⲟϥ·
ⲁⲩ[ⲱ] ⲛⲧⲉⲧⲛ̄ϫⲟⲟⲥ ϫⲉ ⲉ̣ⲓ̣ⲥ̣ ⲡⲉⲕ   21

FOLIO Y
Recto
(ca. 26 lines lost)

- -

→ 91ᶜ   [ⲡⲙⲁ ⲉⲛⲧⲁⲩⲟⲩⲉ]ϩ̣ [ⲛⲁⲩ ⲛϩⲏⲧϥ]   42.27
    [ⲁϥⲛⲁⲩ ⲉⲧⲙⲉⲉ]ⲣⲉ [ⲙ̄ⲡⲉϥϩⲁⲧ ⲁⲩⲱ]
    [ⲛⲉⲥϩⲓϩⲣ]ⲁ̣[ⲥ ⲛⲧ]ϭⲟⲟ[ⲩⲛⲉ ⲡⲉϫⲁϥ ⲛ]   28
    [ⲛⲉϥⲥ]ⲛⲏⲩ ϫⲉ ⲁⲩ[ϯ ⲛⲁⲓ ⲙⲡⲁϩⲁⲧ]
5   [ⲁⲩⲱ] ⲉⲓⲥ ϩⲏⲏⲡⲉ ϥ[ϩⲛ ⲧⲁⲃⲟⲟⲩⲛⲉ]
    [ⲁϥⲡ]ⲱϣ̄ⲥ̄ ⲛ̄ϭⲓ ⲡⲉ[ⲩϩⲏⲧ ⲁⲩⲱ ⲁⲩ]
    [ϣⲧ]ⲟⲣⲧ̄ⲣ ⲉⲩϫⲱ ⲙ̄ⲙ̣[ⲟⲥ ⲛⲛⲉⲩⲉⲣⲏⲩ]
    ϫⲉ ⲟⲩ ⲡⲉ ⲡⲁⲓ̈ ⲉⲛ[ⲧⲁ ⲡⲛⲟⲩⲧⲉ ⲁⲁϥ]
    [ⲛ]ⲁ̣ⲛ̣ ⲁ̣ⲩⲉⲓ ϣⲁ ⲓ̈ⲁ[ⲕⲱⲃ ⲡⲉⲩⲉⲓⲱⲧ]   29
10   [ⲉϩⲣⲁⲓ ⲉ]ⲡⲕⲁϩ ⲛ̄ⲭ[ⲁⲛⲁⲁⲛ ⲁⲩⲭⲱ]
    [ⲉ]ⲣⲟϥ ⲛ̄ϩⲱⲃ ⲛⲓⲙ [ⲉⲛⲧⲁⲩϣⲱⲡⲉ]
    ⲙ̄ⲙⲟⲟⲩ ⲉⲩϫⲱ ⲙ̄ⲙ[ⲟⲥ ϫⲉ ⲁ ⲡⲣⲱ]   30
    ⲙⲉ ϣⲁϫⲉ ⲛⲙ̄ⲙⲁⲛ [ⲡⲭⲟⲉⲓⲥ ⲙ̄]
    ⲡⲕⲁϩ· ⲛ̄ϩⲉⲛϣⲁϫⲉ [ⲉⲩⲛⲁϣⲧ̄]

Verso
(ca. 26 lines lost)

- -

↓ 91ᶜ   [ⲧⲉϥϭⲟⲟⲩⲛ]ⲉ ⲁ̣[ⲩⲛⲁⲩ ⲇⲉ ⲉⲡⲉⲩ]   35
    [ϩⲁⲧ ⲛⲧⲟⲟⲩ ⲙ]ⲛ ⲡ[ⲉⲩⲉⲓⲱⲧ ⲁⲩ]
    [ⲣ ϩⲟⲧⲉ ⲡⲉⲭⲁ]ϥ ⲇⲉ ⲛ̣[ⲁ]ⲩ ⲛ̣[ϭⲓ ⲓⲁ]   36

[ⲕⲱⲃ ⲡⲉⲩⲉⲓⲱ]ⲧ· ϫⲉ ⲁⲧⲉⲧⲛ[ⲁⲁⲧ]
5　[ⲛⲁⲧϣⲏⲣⲉ ⲓ]ⲱⲥⲏⲫ ϣⲟⲟⲡ [ⲁⲛ]
[ⲥⲩⲙⲉⲱⲛ ϣⲟ]ⲟⲡ ⲁⲛ ⲡⲕⲉ[ⲃⲉ]
[ⲛⲓⲁⲙⲓⲛ ⲧ]ⲉⲧⲛ̄ⲛⲁϫⲓⲧϥ̄ ⲛⲁ̣[ⲓ]
[ⲧⲏⲣⲟⲩ ⲛⲧⲁ]ⲩⲉⲓ ⲉϩⲣⲁⲓ̈ ⲉϫⲱ[ⲓ]
[ⲡⲉϫⲉ ϩⲣⲟⲩⲃ]ⲏⲛ ⲇⲉ ⲙ̄ⲡⲉϥ[ⲉⲓⲱⲧ]　　　　37
10　[ⲉϥϫⲱ ⲙⲙⲟⲥ] ϫⲉ ⲙⲟⲩⲟⲩ[ⲧ ⲙ̄ⲡⲁ]
[ϣⲏⲣⲉ ⲥⲛⲁⲩ] ⲉⲉⲓϣⲁⲛⲧⲙ̄[ⲉⲛⲧϥ]
[ϣⲁⲣⲟⲕ † ⲙ]ⲙⲟϥ ⲉϩⲣⲁⲓ̈ ⲉⲛⲁ̣6[ⲓϫ]
[ⲁⲩⲱ ⲁⲛⲟⲕ] †ⲛ̣ⲁⲉⲓⲛⲉ ⲙ̄ⲙⲟϥ ⲉ̣ϩ[ⲣⲁⲓ]
[ϣⲁⲣⲟⲕ ⲛⲧⲟϥ] ⲇⲉ ⲡⲉϫⲁϥ ϫⲉ ⲡⲁϣ[ⲏⲣⲉ]　　38

92	Recto		Verso
	------		------
→	] . ⲉ . [	↓	]ⲉ . [
	------		------

93	Recto		Verso
	------		------
→	]ⲁⲗ[	↓	]†ⲉ[
	------		------

Folio X Recto: (32.5) And he commanded them, saying, "Thus you are going to speak to my lord Esau: thus your servant Jacob says, 'I have dwelt with Laban and have stayed up to today, (6) and there have accrued to me sheep and cattle, male servants and female servants, and I have sent to announce to Esau my lord, in order that your servant may find favor in your presence.'" (7) And the messengers returned to Jacob, saying, "We went to your brother Esau, and behold, he himself is coming to meet you with four hundred men with him. (8) And Jacob became greatly afraid, and he became distressed and divided the people who were with him and the cattle and the sheep into two companies. (9) And Jacob said, "If Esau comes to the first company and slaughters it, the second will be safe." (10) And Jacob said, "God of my father Abraham, and God of my father Isaac, Lord God who said to me, 'Go to the land in which you were born, and I shall do what is good for you,' (11) be a protector for me through all justice and through all truth which you did with your servant; for with my rod I crossed the Jordan, but now I have become two companies. (12)

Save me from the hand of Esau my brother, because for my part I fear him lest he come *Verso*: to strike me and the mothers over their children. (13) And for your part you said to me, 'I am going to do what is good for you, and I am going to make your seed like the sand of the sea, which cannot be counted in its abundance.' " (14) And he slept in that place in that night and took gifts from what he brought and sent them to Esau his brother: (15) two hundred she-goats, twenty he-goats, two hundred sheep, twenty rams, (16) thirty camels who were giving suck to their offspring, forty cattle, ten calves, twenty asses, ten foals, (17) and he gave them through the hands to his servants, each flock apart. And he said to his servants, "Proceed before me and make a separation between flock and flock." (18) And he commanded the first, saying, "If Esau my brother meets you and asks you, saying, 'To whom do you belong, and where are you going, and whose are these which proceed before you?,' (19) you will say to him, 'They are those of your servant Jacob; they are the gifts which he has sent to his lord Esau, and behold, he also follows behind us.' " (20) And he commanded the first and the second and the third and all who followed behind the beasts, saying, "In accordance with this speech will you speak with Esau when you meet him, (21) and you will say, 'Behold, your . . .' "

Folio Y Recto (42.27) . . . the place where they stayed, he saw the bundle of his money, and it was on the mouth of the sack. (28) And he said to his brothers, "My money has been given to me, and behold, it is in my sack." And their heart was amazed, and they were disturbed, saying to one another, "What is this which God has done to us?" (29) And they came to Jacob their father, to the land of Chanaan, and told him everything that had befallen them, saying, (30) "The man, the lord of the land, spoke harsh words with us . . ."

Verso (35) . . . his sack, and they saw their money, themselves and their father, and they became afraid. (36) And Jacob their father said to them, "You have made me childless: Joseph does not exist; Symeon does not exist; even Benjamin you are going to take. It is upon me that all these things have come." (37) And Reuben spoke to his father, saying, "Kill my two sons, if I do not bring him to you. Give him to my hands and for my part I will bring him to you. (38) But for his part he said, "My son . . .".

Folio X Recto

1　ⲁϥϩⲱ[ⲛ ⲉ]ⲧⲟ[ⲟⲧⲟⲩ] K. ⲁϥ is on a piece once folded over on the verso and now lost; only a speck of the ⲁ is visible. The ⲛ of ϩⲱⲛ and the ⲉ of ⲉⲧⲟ[ⲟ]ⲧⲟⲩ are also on a section formerly folded over on the verso and now restored to its proper place.

Note that ⲁϥϩⲱⲛ should be classed as a "hyposyndetic perfect," here corresponding to καὶ ἐνετείλατο in the Greek. Throughout we have used "and" when we translate such perfects.

ⲘⲘⲞⳞ·: a high point, not noted by K, is visible; the fiber alignment shows that it is not an extension of Ⳟ.

4　ⲘⲘⲞⳞ K (sine puncto).

ⲬⲈ: read ⲚϬⲒ; see K ad loc.

8　ϨⲘϨⲀⲖ: ⲁ seems to be corrected from ⲗ; K believes that it was rewritten (see note ad loc. and p. 78).

11　[ⲈⲒⳞ] K. Though faint, Ⳟ followed by a high dot can be discerned under magnification.

12　On the letter, apparently canceled, after ⲈⲂⲞⲖ·, see K p. 78.

13　[Ⲧ]Ⲟ[Ⲩ] ⲚϬⲒ ⲚϤⲀ[ⲒϢ]ⲒⲚⲈ] K; in the case of ϢⲒⲚ, the fibers have been stripped off and only the barest vestiges of ink remain.

14　Ⲙ[ⲘⲞⳞ: only the supralineation remains (cf. K ad loc.).

Ⲛ[ⲈⲔ]: K did not read the ⲚⲦ, of which traces of the horizontal survive.

20 f.　ⲈⲚ[Ⲛ]ⲀⲢⲈⲘⲂⲖⲞⲚ: see K ad loc. and p. 75 n. 12.

21　ⳞⲚⲦⲈ·: there is a faint high dot after Ⲉ, not noted by K.

29　ⲚⲀⲒ K (sine puncto). Of the diaeresis, only the left dot remains.

34　ⲚⲈⲔϨⲘ· K; there are faint traces after ⲙ, but they may only be smudges of ink.

35　[Ϩ]ⲀⲖ· [Ϩ]ⲠⲀⲒ K.

36　[Ⲁ]ⲒⲬⲒⲞⲞⲢ K.

39　The stroke over the final ⲁ is not recorded in K's text, but he mentions it on p. 79.

Verso

1　Ⲙ[Ⲙ]ⲀⲀⲨ K.

1 f.　[Ϩ]/ⲠⲀⲒ, K's reading, is perhaps better suited to the lacuna; but with [ⲈϨ]/ⲠⲀⲒ, line 1 would be no longer than line 7, the text would conform to Ceugney and Ciasca, and the word division would be unobjectionable (cf. ⲈϨ/ⲠⲀⲒ in X R 29 f.).

9　[ϨⲚ] K.

10 ɴє[[т]]ɴтλq-: for the cancellation of the т, see K p. 79.
λqхооγ[соγ]: or λqхооγ[сє] (see K ad loc.).

11 м̄вλ K; in this hand, it is at times hard to distinguish between м and ɴ, but we should prefer to read ɴ̄вλ (for the form, cf. the first letter of ɴ̄сλ in line 37 below). Unfortunately, the text provides no other instance of ɴ̄ + в.

12 х[о]γϣт K.

13 м[λ] K.

14 Only the supralineation is visible in the case of the last two ɴ's in this line (so K ad loc.).

15 ϩмн K; Ciasca has ϩмє.

18 ɴ[бιх] ɴ̣ɴ̣ᴇ[qϩ]мϩλλ· K.

21 ɴ̄ɴ̣оγ: see K ad loc.

24 єр: the є seems to have been corrected from р (not noted by K).

26 ɴq̄хɴоγ̄к K; but there is no stroke over the γ: the fibers are damaged so as to give the impression of supralineation.

28 єтωɴ·: the high dot, which is almost completely invisible except under magnification, was not reported by K.

30 [ос] K.

30 f. ῑ/ιλ[кωв ɴє ɴλ]ωроɴ K; for the word division, see K p. 75 n. 12.

33 ϩннпє·: K does not record the very faint point.

35 пмᴇγсɴλ̄γ: i.e. пмᴇϩсɴλγ; see K ad loc.

36 пмᴇϩϣомт̄: the first м was added above the line (so K); K reads a high dot after т, but we cannot discern it on the original.

37 ɴ[ιм] K.

39 [єт]єтɴ̄ᴇϣλхᴇ K.

40 [пт]р̣ᴇтᴇтɴтωмт K.

41 ɴ]тᴇтɴ̄хоос K.
   є̣ι̣ç̣: written over ɴλ? (see K ad loc.)

Folio Y Recto

1 [мпмλ (є)ɴтλγоγн]ϩ̣ K; there seems to be insufficient room for м at the beginning of the line unless ɴтλγ- is read; but єɴтλγ- would correspond to the spelling elsewhere found in the text (X R 30, 34; Y R 8). The form оγнϩ should be corrected to оγєϩ; for the expression оγєϩ ɴλ⸗, see Crum, *Dict.* 506b.

2 тмᴇᴇ]р̣ᴇ: so K; for the form, see his *Compléments* ad 182a. The р, however, is most uncertain and appears to resemble rather

a ϩ; but we have been unable to find a Coptic word ending in -ϩⲉ
and corresponding to the Greek, which here has εἶδεν τὸν δεσμόν.

3   ϩⲣ]ⲁ̣[ⲥ: this is entirely in a lacuna in K's transcript.

5   ϥ[ϩⲛ: though damaged, ϥ appears to be certain, despite K's
reservations in his note ad loc.

7   ⲙ̅[ⲙⲟⲥ K.

9   Presumably after [ⲛ]ⲁ̣ⲛ̣ there was a mark of punctuation
which can no longer be recovered, followed by a space for one letter,
then by ⲁⲅⲉⲓ. K prints [ⲛ]ⲁ̣ⲛ̣ [. ⲁ]ⲅⲉⲓ.

12   [ⲙⲙ]ⲟⲟⲩ K; of the first ⲙ only the supralinear stroke
survives.

ⲁⲡ(ⲓ)ⲣⲱ]ⲙⲉ K; apparently in his entertaining the possibility of
ⲡⲓ, he was overly influenced by the Bohairic, which here has
ⲡⲓⲣⲱⲙⲓ.

13   At the end of the line, K prints [(ⲉⲧⲉ) ⲡⲭⲟⲉⲓⲥ (ⲡⲉ) ⲙ].
With ⲉⲧⲉ and ⲡⲉ, the restoration would be too long, and consequently we have preferred the shorter [ⲡⲭⲟⲉⲓⲥ ⲙ], which corres-
ponds to the Bohairic (ⲡϭⲥ ⲙⲡⲓⲕⲁϩⲓ).

14   K prints [ⲉⲩⲛⲁϣⲧ (ⲁⲩⲱ)], but there is probably not
enough room for the conjunction.

Verso

1   [ⲁⲩⲛⲁⲩ K.

4   ⲡⲉⲩ(ⲉ)ⲓⲱ]ⲧ· K; presumably he thought the full spelling
would be slightly too long for the space available, but we believe
that the lacuna can accomodate ⲉⲓⲱⲧ, which is also the form
found elsewhere in the text (X R 26 and 28).

7   [ⲛⲁⲓ] K.

8   [ⲧⲏⲣⲟⲩ (ⲛⲧ)ⲁ]ⲅⲉⲓ K; of the two witnesses to this text,
one reads ⲁⲅⲉⲓ, and ⲁⲅⲉⲓ is restored in the other (cf. K ad loc.).
With the first perfect, the restoration is too short; the second
perfect, which suits the space available, effectively renders the
emphasis implicit in the Greek (ἐπ' ἐμὲ ἐγένετο πάντα ταῦτα).

ⲉ̣[ⲭⲱⲓ] K.

13   ϯⲛ̣ⲁ-: ⲛ corrected from ⲕ?

3 HOMILY OR EPISTLE

Inv. VII 100ᶜ: 8 × 8.1 cm.

This text is written in a careful uncial hand; the ⲁ at times has a
peculiar form, with a long and almost vertical tail.

The content is somewhat puzzling; the text is cast in homiletical or epistolary form, but the absence of customary formulas seems to make it unlikely that it is a personal letter like the others in cover VII. The fact, however, that the verso is blank suggests that it is not from a literary codex. Perhaps it is a copy of an individual homily or letter from a person in high authority circulated to monastic communities. The text evidently exhorts its readers to the pursuit of virtue; the last line may well have contained a citation from a prophet, but the reading is uncertain. For the suggestion that the text may have been written by Pachomius, see Introd. 10-11.

→

```
     ]N2NCNHY 2M ΠNEYMA T . [
     ]ΑΙΤΙΑ 2M ΠΙCTPAHΛ EΑY . [
     ] . TBBHY EΘBBIHHY EΘN . [
     ] . ΛEΙOYWϢE W NCNHY 2[
  5  NTE]PICΖAEI NHTN XE ϢWΠE N[
     ] . . . ΠWT NCWq NTETNΠϢ[T
     Π]WT EBOΛ 2M ΠEΘΑY MN Π[
     N]TΑ NEΠPOΦHTEIA MΠNO[YTE
     ]CAΖOY . CEKONAΘPOCΖ . [
```
- -

1 ΖEN-; last letter in line either O or W   2 ΠICPAHΛ   3 Of the first letter only a faint speck remains: perhaps P or Ζ (E]TTBBHY cannot be read); ETΘBBIHY   4 First letter: I, H, N, or Π; not E; -OYWϢ; NECNHY   6 Probably M]ΠEPΠWT   7 ΠEΘOOY   9 After Y, apparently a high horizontal, e.g. T; at end of line Ζ could also be read as B.

... brothers in spirit ... cause in Israel ... pure, who are (?) humble ... I wished, o brothers ... when (?) I wrote to you, saying "be ... do not (?) run after it (?) and run ... run from evil and ... which the prophecies of God ...

4 LETTER OF DANIEL TO APHRODISI(OS)

5 LETTER OF APHRODISI(OS) TO SANSNOS

Inv. VII 94ᶜ: 16.2 × 21 cm.; 95ᶜ: 2.3 × 2.4 cm.; 96ᶜ: 1.5 × 1 cm.

These two letters are written, along the fibers, on both sides of a nearly complete sheet of papyrus of fair quality. Photographs taken at the preliminary stage of separating the contents of this cover show parts of the recto text subsequently lost; these have been incorporated in the photographic reproduction in pl. 51 of *The Facsimile Edition of the Nag Hammadi Codices: Cartonnage* (Leiden 1979).

The text on the recto (4), a letter from Daniel to Aphrodisi(os), is in a crude style in terms of orthography; but the composition is grammatical and competent, and there are only a few serious spelling errors, though we find occasional lapses from the correct Sahidic at which the writer evidently aims. He expresses concern at the recent illness of his correspondent, and relief at the news that he is on the way to recovery, with an apt quotation from the Epistle to the Hebrews. The letter ends with expressions of loyal affection for Aphrodisios and the hope that the writer will be reunited with him. Both sender and recipient are evidently members of religious communities, and the latter, who is perhaps identical with the Aphrodisios mentioned in Greek text **69**, [1] is addressed in terms of high regard and would appear to have been of some standing; this fact makes the standard of literacy shown by the text on the verso the more surprising. Someone—presumably Aphrodisios himself—has defaced the writing on the recto by scratching it out with his pen and has made several blots.

The text on the verso (5) is a letter from Aphrodisios himself; its addressee, despite the variant spelling of his name, may be the Sansnos with whom much of the correspondence from cover VII is concerned.[2] It is written in very large, square, thick letters, labored and badly spaced; the impression it gives of semi-literacy is amply borne out by its atrocious spelling and grammatical aberrancies, which in more than one place make interpretation uncertain. We therefore first give a purely diplomatic transcription, to which we then add an attempt at a correct text of all but the fragmentary last line; it is upon this second text that the tentative translation rests. It appears that Aphrodisios asks Sansnos to postpone the dispatch of some wheat which he has requested, since he is too ill to deal with the matter; in fact, he does not know whether he will survive. He also gives instructions about some money transactions.

We have not been able to place the tiny fragment catalogued as inv. VII 96ᶜ. It is too small to warrant transcription.

---

[1] But see Introd. 9.
[2] See Introd. 7-9.

4

→ ⲇⲁ̣[ⲛⲓ]ⲏ̣ⲗ ⲡⲉⲧⲥϩⲁⲓ̈ ⲙⲡⲉϥⲙⲉⲣⲓⲧ ⲛⲛⲉⲓ̣ⲱⲧ̣ ⲁ̣ⲫ[ⲣ]ⲟ̣ϯⲥ̣ⲓ̣ [ϩⲙ]
ⲡϫⲟⲉ̣ⲓ̣ⲥ· ⲭⲁⲓⲣⲉ: ϩⲁⲑⲏ ⲛϩⲱⲃ ⲛⲓⲙ ϯϣⲓⲛⲉ ⲉⲣⲟⲕ [ⲙⲛ]
ⲛⲉⲥⲛⲏⲟⲩ· ⲧⲏⲣⲟⲩ· ⲉⲧϣⲟⲟⲡ· ϩⲁⲧⲏⲕ· ⲕⲁⲧⲁ ⲛⲉⲩⲣ[ⲁⲛ ⲟⲩⲁ]
ⲟⲩⲁ: ⲧⲉⲛⲟⲩ ϭⲉ: ⲡⲁϫⲟⲉⲓⲥ ⲛⲛⲉⲓⲱⲧ ⲕⲱ ⲛⲛⲁⲕ̣ ⲉ̣ⲃⲟⲗ̣ [ⲙ]
ⲡⲉⲕϩⲏⲧ· ⲧⲏⲣϥ· ⲁ̣ⲓ̈ⲥⲱⲧⲙ· ⲅⲁⲣ ϫ̣ⲉ̣ ⲁⲕϣ̣ⲱ̣ⲛ̣ⲉ̣ ϩ̣[ⲛ ⲟⲩⲛⲟϭ]
ⲛϣⲱⲛ̣ⲉ̣· ⲁ ⲡ̣ⲁ̣ϩ̣ⲏ̣[ⲧ ⲙ]ⲕⲁ̣ϩ· ⲉ̣ⲙ̣[ⲁⲧⲉ . . . . . .] . [
. . . . [. . . . .] . . [.] . . [
[ϩ]ⲟ̣ⲙ̣ⲱ̣ⲥ̣ ⲇⲉ ⲁⲛⲟⲕ· ⲟⲩϭⲱⲃ ⲛⲧⲁⲗⲁⲓⲡⲱⲣⲟⲥ ⲛⲣ̣[ⲉϥⲣ] ⲛⲟ̣[ⲃⲉ]
ⲙⲡⲓⲙϣⲁ· ⲁⲧⲣⲉ ⲡⲛⲟⲩⲧⲉ: ⲕⲁⲁⲧ: ⲉ̣ⲧ̣ⲉⲓⲥⲙⲟⲧ̣ . . [
ⲛⲓⲙ: ⲡⲛⲟⲩⲧⲉ· ⲡⲉⲧⲥⲟⲟⲩⲛ· ⲡⲉⲧϩⲙ ⲫⲏⲧ· ⲛ̄ⲛⲟⲩ . . . . [
ϫⲉ ⲛⲧⲁⲣⲉⲓⲥⲱⲧⲙ ⲁ ⲡⲁϩⲏⲧ· ⲙⲕⲁϩ ⲉⲉⲓϣ̣ⲓ̣ⲛ̣ⲉ̣ ϭⲛ̣ [ⲡⲉⲕ]
ⲟⲩⲱ ⲉⲡⲓⲇⲏ· ⲛⲕⲟ̣ⲩⲉ̣ ⲉ̣ⲧ̣ⲙ̣ ⲡⲏⲓ ⲉⲧⲛⲉ̣ⲙⲙⲉ ⲇ̣ⲓⲁ[
ⲉ̣ⲩⲣ ϣⲁⲩ· ⲕⲁⲗⲟⲥ· ⲧⲉⲛⲟⲩ ϭⲉ ⲉⲣ̣ⲉ ⲡ̣[ⲉ]ⲕ̣ⲟⲩⲱ· ⲛⲁⲗⲟ̣ ⲉ̣[
ⲙ̣ⲙ̣ⲟⲕ: ⲁϥⲧ̣ⲉ̣ⲕ̣ ⲡⲁϩⲏⲧ ⲉⲙⲁⲧⲉ [ⲉ]ⲡⲉⲧⲓ̣ϣ̣ⲓ̣ⲛ̣ⲉ ⲛ̣[ⲥⲱϥ]
ⲉ̣ⲉⲓⲟⲩⲱϣⲉ· ⲉϭ̣ⲛ· ⲡⲉⲕⲟⲩⲱ· ⲧⲉⲛⲟⲩ ϭ̣ⲉ ⲡⲁϫ̣ⲟⲉ̣ⲓ̣ⲥ̣ [ⲛⲛ]
ⲉⲓⲱⲧ ⲉⲡⲓⲇⲏ ⲉⲁ ⲡⲁϫⲟⲉⲓⲥ ⲛⲥⲟⲛ· ⲥⲟⲩⲣⲟⲩⲥ̣ ⲧⲁ[ⲙⲟⲓ]
ϫⲉ ⲁⲕⲧⲓ ⲁⲧϩ̣ⲏ̣· ⲁ ⲡⲁϩⲏⲧ ⲙⲙⲧⲟⲛ ⲉ̣ϥⲥⲏϩ ⲅ̣ⲁ̣ⲣ ϫⲉ [ⲡⲉⲧⲉ]
ⲣⲉ ⲡϫⲟⲉⲓⲥ ⲙⲉ ⲙⲙⲟϥ ϣⲁϥⲡⲉⲇⲉⲩⲉ ⲙⲙⲟ[ϥ] ϣⲁϥ̣[ⲙⲁⲥ]
ⲧⲓⲕⲟⲩ· ⲛϣⲏⲣⲉ ⲛⲓⲙ ⲉⲧϥⲛⲁϣⲟⲟⲡⲟⲩⲓ ⲉⲣⲟϥ [ⲉ]ⲡ̣ⲓ̈ⲇ̣ⲏ̣ [ⲡⲁ]
ⲙⲉⲣⲓⲧ· ⲁ ⲡⲛⲟⲩⲧⲉ ⲧⲟⲩⲛⲟⲥⲕ ⲅ̣ϫⲁⲕⲁⲙ̣ ϩⲙ ⲡ̣[. .]ⲛⲟ . [
ⲛⲟⲃⲉ: ⲉⲉⲓⲉ· ⲧⲱⲕ· ⲛϩⲏⲧ ⲛⲧⲁⲱϩⲉ· ⲉⲣⲁⲧ·[. .]ⲧ . [
ϯϩⲉⲗⲡⲓⲥ ⲉⲡⲛⲟⲩⲧⲉ ϫⲉ ⲥⲉⲛⲁⲧⲁⲧ ⲛⲙ̣ⲁ̣ⲕ· ⲁⲣ̣[ⲓ ϩ]ⲙⲟⲧ [ⲛⲅ]
ⲛⲉϫ ϣⲗⲏⲗ ⲛ̄ⲛⲧⲟⲕ ⲙⲛ̄ ⲛⲉⲕⲙⲁⲕ[ⲁⲣⲓⲟⲥ ⲛⲥⲟ]ⲛ̣ ⲉ̣[ⲧϣ]
ⲟⲟⲡ· ϩⲁⲧⲏⲕ· ⲧ̣ⲉⲛⲟⲩ ϭⲉ ⲛⲁⲙⲉⲣ̣[ⲁⲧⲉ
ϩⲛ ⲛⲉⲧⲛϣⲗⲏⲗ ⲛⲁϫⲓⲥⲟⲟⲩⲉ· ⲛⲁⲥ̣ . [. . .] . . [
ⲙ̣ⲁ̣ ⲛⲧⲁϫⲣⲟ ⲙⲛⲥⲁ ⲡⲛⲟⲩⲧⲉ̣ ϯⲧⲏ̣[ⲧ ⲛ]ϩⲏⲧ̣ [
ⲙ̣ⲙⲁ ϩⲙ ⲡⲕⲟⲥⲙⲟⲥ· ⲉⲛϣⲁⲉⲓ ϭⲉ ⲉⲕ[ⲛⲁ]ϣ̣ⲱⲡⲉ̣ [ϩ]
ⲙⲟⲧ ϯⲛⲁⲱⲛϩ ϫ[. . ϩⲙ] ⲡϫⲟⲉⲓⲥ̣

1 ⲛⲉⲓⲱⲧ; ⲁⲫⲣⲟⲇⲓⲥⲓ(ⲟⲥ) 4 ⲛⲉⲓⲱⲧ; ⲛⲁⲕ 9 ⲙⲡⲓⲙⲡϣⲁ ⲉⲧⲣⲉ 10 ⲛ̄ⲛⲟⲩ: ⲛ² added above the line 11 ⲛⲧⲉⲣⲓ-; -ϣⲓⲛⲉ ⲉϭⲛ 12 ⲛⲕⲟⲟⲩⲉ ⲉⲧϩⲙ; ⲉⲧⲛⲙⲙⲁⲓ 13 ⲕⲁⲗⲱⲥ 15 -ⲟⲩⲱϣ 15 f. ⲛⲉⲓⲱⲧ 17 ⲉⲑⲏ; ⲙⲧⲟⲛ 18 -ⲡⲁⲓⲇⲉⲩⲉ 18 f. -ⲙⲁⲥⲧⲓⲅⲟⲩ 19 ⲉⲧϥⲛⲁϣⲟⲡⲟⲩ 20 ⲕϫⲟⲕⲙ 22 ϯϩⲉⲗⲡⲓⲍⲉ (see note ad loc.); -ⲧⲁⲁⲧ ⲛⲙⲙⲁⲕ 23 ⲛⲧⲟⲕ 26 ⲙⲛⲛⲥⲁ 27 ⲉⲛϣⲁⲛⲉⲓ (see note ad loc.)

It is Daniel who writes to his beloved father Aphrodisi(os), in the Lord, greetings. Before everything I greet you and all the brothers who are with you, each by name. Now then, my lord father, be relieved with your whole heart. For I heard that you fell sick with a serious sickness, and my heart was much grieved . . . But nevertheless I am a wretched, sinful weakling; I was not worthy that God should set me in this role. [For] who [am I?] It is God who knows what is in the heart [of everyone.] For when I heard, my heart was grieved, while I sought to get news of you, since the others who are in the house with me continue (?) to be greatly benefited. Now, therefore, since news of you will . . . you, it cheered my heart greatly concerning what I was searching after, desiring to get news of you. Now, therefore, my lord father, since my lord brother Sourous has told me that you have improved, my heart has been relieved. For it is written: "Whom the Lord loves, he is wont to chastise; he scourges every son whom he will receive to himself." Since, my beloved, God has raised you up, you are cleansed by the sin[less blood]; then be of good cheer, and I shall stand [with you, for] I put my hope in God that I shall be set with you. Have the goodness to send up prayers, both you and your blessed brothers who are with you. Now, therefore, my beloved [brothers, remember me] in your prayers; my [ascetic] lords, [you are our] strong refuge, after God. I am convinced [that if we are in any] place in the world, when we then come, you will become [a] blessing [for me], and I shall live. Be [strong] in the Lord.

1 ⲁⲁ̣[ⲛⲓ]ⲏ̣ⲗ: despite damage and cancellation, the restoration seems certain; ⲁⲁ̣[ⲟⲩ]ⲉ̣ⲓ̣ⲁ̣ cannot be read.

4 f. ⲕⲱ ⲛⲛⲁⲕ̣ ⲉ̣ⲃⲟⲗ̣ [ⲙ]ⲡⲉⲕϩⲏⲧ: see Crum, *Dict.* 715b for comparable expressions.

9 f. Perhaps ⲁ̣ⲛ̣[ⲟⲕ ⲅⲁⲣ ⲁⲛⲅ] ⲛⲓⲙ, "For who am I?" But ⲛⲓⲙ might not be interrogative, but indefinite: "any."

10 At the end of the line perhaps {ⲛ}ⲛⲟⲩⲟ̣ⲛ̣ ⲛ̣ⲓ̣[ⲙ], "of everyone."

12 Perhaps ⲁ̣ⲓⲁ[ⲧⲉⲗⲉⲓ], "continue."

16 For Sourous, see Introd. 9.

17-19 The quote is from Hebr. 12.6.

20 f. Perhaps ϩⲙ ⲡ̣[ⲉⲥ]ⲛⲟϥ [ⲛⲁⲧ]ⲛⲟⲃⲉ, "by the sinless blood."

21 At end, perhaps [ϩⲁ]ⲧⲏ̣[ⲕ ϫⲉ], "with you, for . . ."

22 ϯϩⲉⲗⲡⲓⲥ: i.e. ϯϩⲉⲗⲡⲓⲍⲉ; the use of a Greek noun in place of a verb is not uncommon in Coptic; compare the following examples from E. A. E. Raymond and J. W. B. Barns, *Four*

Martyrdoms from the Pierpont Morgan Coptic Codices (Oxford 1973): Paese and Thecla 51 R i 29 f. ⲃⲟⲏⲑⲓⲁ ⲉⲣⲟⲓ (see edd.'s note ad loc.), Shenoufe 112 V i 7 ⲛϥⲧⲣⲉⲩⲑⲩⲥⲓⲁ (which, despite the edd.'s note, need not be corrected to -ⲣ ⲑⲩⲥⲓⲁ), Shenoufe 120 V ii 32 ⲁϥⲃⲟⲏⲑⲓⲁ ⲉⲣⲟⲛ, Colluthus II (App.) 17 v i 19 f. ⲛϯⲭⲣⲓⲁ ⲙⲙⲟⲟⲩ ⲁⲛ (which the edd. needlessly emend to -ⲣ ⲭⲣⲓⲁ).

24 Perhaps ⲛⲁⲙⲉⲣ[ⲁⲧⲉ ⲛⲥⲟⲛ ⲁⲣⲓ ⲡⲁⲙⲉⲉⲩⲉ], "my beloved brothers, remember me."

25 Possibly ⲛⲁ̣ⲥ̣ⲕ̣[ⲓⲧⲏ]ⲥ̣ ⲛ̣[ⲧⲉⲧⲛ ⲡⲉⲛ-], ". . . ascetic, you are our . . ."

26 At end perhaps [ⲭⲉ ⲉⲛ̅ⲛ ⲗⲁⲁⲩ], ". . . that if we are in any . . ."

27 ⲉⲛ(ϣ)ⲁⲉⲓ: for the form of the conditional, see **2** X R 22, and Kasser's comments in "Fragments du livre biblique de la Genèse cachés dans la reliure d'un codex gnostique", *Le Muséon* 85 (1972) 83.

At end possibly [ⲛⲁⲓ ⲛⲟⲩⲥ]/ⲙⲟⲧ, "a blessing for me."

28 The last words are written large; probably ⲭ[ⲣⲟ ⲛⲙ] ⲡⲭⲟⲉⲓⲥ̣ "be strong in the Lord."

5

→

```
    .ⲁⲡⲣⲟϯⲥⲉⲡⲉⲅⲉⲓⲛ̣ⲭⲁⲛⲥⲛⲉⲟⲩⲥⲛⲭⲁⲉⲓⲥⲭⲉ[
     ⲭⲉⲣⲉⲅⲁⲑⲏⲛⲅⲃⲛⲓⲙϯϣⲓⲛⲉⲁⲣⲁⲕⲙ[[ⲓ]]ⲛⲛⲉⲧ
     ⲛⲙⲉⲕⲭ̣ⲉ̣ⲉⲧⲧⲃⲉⲛⲕ̣ⲟⲩⲉⲓⲛⲥⲟⲩⲟⲛⲁⲁ[
     ⲭⲟⲥⲛⲉⲕⲉⲧⲃⲏⲧⲟⲩⲭⲉⲧⲁⲟⲩⲥⲉⲁⲣⲓⲡ.[
5    ⲧⲟⲣⲅⲙⲉ(ϣ)ⲁⲛϯⲧⲛ ⲛⲁⲟⲩⲛⲅⲱⲟⲩⲭⲉ[
     ϯ(ϣ)ⲱⲛⲉⲁⲅⲛⲭⲱⲙⲉⲭⲓⲭⲟⲩⲭⲁⲙⲁⲉ[
     ϭⲓϭⲱⲣ·ⲛⲁⲟⲟⲧ.ϥⲛⲛⲁⲃⲣⲁⲙϯⲙⲏⲧ[
     ⲙⲱⲥⲛⲥϯⲥⲁⲟⲩⲛⲁⲡ'ⲟⲗⲟⲛⲅⲏⲧ..[
     ⲭⲉϯⲥⲁⲟⲩⲛⲉⲛⲭⲉ.ⲩⲡⲉⲧⲛ̅ⲁ̇(ϣ)ⲱⲡⲉ[̣
10   ⲛⲙⲁⲉⲓⲉ|ⲁⲉ.ⲉⲉⲓⲅⲛⲡ(ϣ)ⲱⲙ·ⲁ'ⲉⲗⲁⲉⲉⲓⲱ̅ⲛ[
     ⲛⲉ.ⲃⲁ........ⲉ̣ⲙⲉⲁⲩ.[
```

1 The line begins with what appears to be merely a blot, but if so, it was made before the letter was written, since the writing begins a little to the right. 4 At end: ⲉ, ⲑ, ⲟ, ⲥ, or ⲱ 7 ⲛⲁⲟⲟⲧ. ϥ: ⲧ added above the line 8 Last two letters probably ⲟⲩ 9 ⲭⲉ added in left margin 10 ⲉⲓⲁⲉ.: after ⲉ² perhaps ⲟ corrected to ⲉ, or ⲟ canceled

ⲁⲫⲣⲟⲇⲓⲥ(ⲓⲟⲥ) ⲡⲉⲧⲥⲅⲁⲓ ⲛⲥⲁⲛⲥⲛⲱⲥ ⲅⲙ ⲡⲭⲟⲉⲓⲥ {ⲭⲉ} ⲭⲁⲓⲣⲉ. ⲅⲁⲑⲏ ⲛⲅⲱⲃ ⲛⲓⲙ ϯϣⲓⲛⲉ ⲉⲣⲟⲕ ⲙⲛ ⲛⲉⲧ ⲛⲙⲙⲁⲕ· ⲭⲉ (?) ⲉⲧⲃⲉ ⲛⲕⲟⲩⲓ ⲛⲥⲟⲩⲟ ⲛⲧⲁⲓ

ⲭⲟⲟⲥ ⲛⲁⲕ ⲉⲧⲃⲏⲏⲧⲟⲩ ⲭⲉ ⲧⲟⲟⲩⲥⲉ, ⲁⲣⲓ ⲡ . [
5   ⲧⲟⲣ̅ⲅⲙⲉ (?) ϣⲁⲛⲧⲧⲛⲛⲟⲟⲩ ⲛⲥⲱⲟⲩ, ⲭⲉ
ⲧϣⲱⲛⲉ ⲉⲅⲉⲛϭⲱⲱⲙⲉ (?). ⲭⲓ ⲭⲟⲩⲧⲁϥⲧⲉ [ⲛ]
ϭⲓⲛϭⲱⲣ ⲛⲧⲟⲟⲧϥ ⲛⲁⲃⲣⲁⲅⲁⲙ· ϯ ⲙⲏⲧ [ⲙ]
ⲙⲱⲩⲥⲏⲥ {ϯⲥⲟⲟⲩⲛ} ⲉⲃⲟⲗ ⲛ̅ⲅⲏⲧⲟⲩ·
ⲭⲉ ϯⲥⲟⲟⲩⲛ ⲁⲛ ⲭⲉ ⲟⲩ ⲡⲉⲧⲛⲁϣⲱⲡⲉ
10   ⲙⲙⲟⲓ, ⲉⲓⲧⲉ ⲉⲓⲉⲉⲓ ⲅⲙ ⲡⲥⲱⲙⲁ ⲉⲓⲧⲉ ⲉⲓⲉⲱⲛ[ⲅ]

It is Aphrodis(ios) who writes to Sansnos, in the Lord, greetings.
Before everything, I greet you and those with you. Concerning
the small quantities of wheat concerning which I said to you,
"buy them," . . . until I send for them, because I am sick with
cramps (?). Take twenty-four talents from Abraham; give ten to
Moses {I know} out of them. For I do not know what is going to
befall me, whether I shall come out of the body or I shall live . . .

1   ⲍⲁⲛⲥⲛⲉⲟⲩⲥ: doubtless a writing of the common name
ⲥⲁⲛⲥⲛⲱⲥ.

3   ⲭⲉ: apparently redundant; perhaps an ellipse is involved:
"[know] that . . ."

4 f.   The end of line 4 and the beginning of 5 yield no obvious
sense. Perhaps ⲁⲣⲓ ⲡⲉ[ⲅⲙⲟ]ⲧ ⲟⲩⲱⲣ̅ⲅ (for ⲟⲩⲱ̅ⲅⲣ) ⲙⲙⲟⲟⲩ,
"be good enough to set them aside." ⲟⲩⲱⲣ̅ⲅ, "set free, open,
renounce" (cf. Dem. wrḥ, "set free, admit") and ⲟⲩⲱ̅ⲅⲣ, "put
aside, save, spare?" (possibly to be equated with wḥr, "take care
of, provide") [1] seem at times to have interchanged; cf. Ryl 368 n. 6.
For the spelling without ⲟⲩ-, cf. BKU III 403.4 and 10 ⲁⲓⲟⲣⲉⲅϥ.

6   ⲧϣⲱⲛⲉ ⲁⲅⲛ̅ⲭⲱⲙⲉ (= ⲉⲅⲉⲛϭⲱⲱⲙⲉ?): the interpretation of this phrase is very doubtful. If ϭⲱⲱⲙⲉ is right, it should
mean something like "cramps"; the meaning "perversion" listed
in Crum, Dict. 818a is hardly appropriate.

8   It seems likely that ϯⲥⲁⲟⲩⲛ is here mistakenly written in
anticipation of the same word in the next line.

10   At the beginning of the line, the writer seems to intend
ⲛⲙⲙⲁⲓ, but this itself appears to be a mistake for ⲙⲙⲟⲓ. ⲙⲙⲟ⸗
is regularly used with ϣⲱⲡⲉ in the sense of "befall, happen to"
(Crum, Dict. 578b).

ⲉⲉⲓⲅⲛ̅ⲡϣⲱⲙ·ⲁ (= ⲉⲓ ⲅⲙ ⲡⲥⲱⲙⲁ), "to come out of the body,"
is one of the many euphemisms for "to die."

_____

[1] See J. Černý, Coptic Etymological Dictionary (Cambridge 1976) 216 and
223.

6 LETTER OF PAPNOUTE (PAPNOUTIOS) TO PAHOME (PACHOMIOS)

7 LETTER OF PAPNOUTE

Inv. VII 97ᶜ (**6**): 12.6 × 15.2 cm.; 98ᶜ (**7**): 7.5 × 7 cm.; 99ᶜ: 1.5 × 1 cm.

We here publish two large fragments, with a small scrap (Inv. VII 99ᶜ) which might belong to either. Although the two main pieces are plainly in the same hand, a large, rather clumsy semi-cursive, they can hardly belong to the same document, since, if they did, the writing on one side might be taken to run in three different directions.[1] In **7** we cannot determine which side was written first, and consequently we designate the two surfaces simply as "a" and "b" rather than "recto" and "verso." It may be remarked that in **7** a 5-7 the writer seems to be discussing the same matter as in **6**.13 ff.; in both places a conversation is reported. In both fragments the body of the letter is continued on the verso; in **6**, however, there is also an address on the verso, which, if our reading of it is correct, furnishes a significant indication of the identity of the addressee, and consequently of the sender and perhaps the other individuals mentioned in **6** and **7**. It is tempting to assume, though it cannot be proven, that **6** is addressed to the great Pachomios himself by his *oikonomos* Papnoutios, the writer of both of these letters. But see above, Introd. 10-11.

Apart from the introductory formula, too much of the body of each letter has been lost to enable us to gather much about the contents. The orthography is quite good, and the dialect pure Sahidic.

6

→ ΜΠΑΜΕΝΡΙΤ Ν̄ΙΩΤ ΠΑϨΩΜΕ
    ΠΑΠΝΟΥΤΕ ϨΝ̄ ΠΧΟΕΙⲤ ΧΕΡΕ
    ϨΑΘΗ Ν̄Ϩ[Ω]Β ΝΙΜ ϮϢΙΝΕ ΕΡΟΚ
    Μ̄ΠΟ[ΟΥ ϮϢΙ]ΝΕ ΕΠΑⲤΟΝ Η . [
5   [.] . [Ν̄ϮΜ]ΠϢΑ ΠΑΜΕΝΡΙΤ
    [ΝΙΩΤ . . .] . ΕϢΙΝΕ ΕΡΩΤΝ̄
    [ⲓ]ΩΤ ΜΑΚΑΡΙ ϮΝΟ . [

---

[1] See Plate 54 of *The Facsimile Edition of the Nag Hammadi Codices: Cartonnage* (Leiden 1979).

```
      [              ] . ⲧ ⲙⲙⲉⲣⲓⲧ ⲧⲓ
      [              ] ⲛⲁⲕ ⲭⲉ ⲕ̣ⲭⲱ
10    [              ] . [ . ]ⲡⲁⲓ ⲉϥⲛⲁⲓ
      [              ] ⲙ̄ⲛ ⲡⲉⲉⲓ
      [              ]ϣⲱⲥⲗⲁⲩ
      [              ]ϣⲱⲥⲙ̄
      [              ]ⲉⲙⲉϥ† ϲⲟ
15    [              ] ⲁⲗⲗⲁ ⲡⲉⲭⲁϥ
      [              ]ⲉⲩⲙ̄ⲡⲉⲧ[
      [              ]ⲑⲉⲟⲥ ⲛ̄ϩⲟ[
      [              ]ⲱⲛ̄ⲟⲡ[
      [              ]ⲛ̣ⲉ̣[
```

Verso   --------------------

↓   ] . ⲓⲥ . [
             ]ⲙ̄ⲡϣⲁ[
             ]ⲛ̄ⲧⲉ[ⲓ]ϭ̣[ⲟ]ⲧ̣[
             ] . ⲛⲟⲩϣⲓⲛ . [
5   ] . . ⲧⲉ . . [

Address

→   ] . ⲁⲡⲣ̣[.] . ⲏ†[. .]⁻ ⲉⲓⲱⲧ
                    ]ⲧⲉ . [

1 ff. It would appear that each of the first four lines at least began a little to the right of the preceding.   2-5 There are traces of ink before the beginning of each line; they are perpendicular to the writing, and perhaps the scribe continued the letter in the margin; opposite line 5 an ⲁ seems secure:] ⲁ [.]. etc.   2 Over the ⲭ of ⲭⲉⲣⲉ a blot   4 At end, very faint traces after ⲏ   5 At end, another blot   8 At beginning, before ⲧ, a stroke, low, apparently not part of ⲱ; perhaps fortuitous. At end, no certain traces after ⲧⲓ   10 First letter an upright, perhaps ⲓ
    Verso   1 Perhaps ⲭⲟ]ⲉ̣ⲓⲥ ⲛ̣[Address   1 At beginning, before ⲁ, perhaps ⲡ or ⲙ   2 After ⲧⲉ perhaps merely a blot?

1-7 These lines may be translated: "To my beloved father, Pahome, Papnoute, in the Lord, greetings. Before everything I greet you today; I greet my brother E--- . . . I am not worthy, my beloved father . . . to greet you . . . father Makari(os) . . ."

    5 [ⲛ†ⲙ]ⲡϣⲁ: perhaps the negative particle ⲁⲛ was inadvertently omitted after ⲛ†ⲙⲡϣⲁ.

    7 ⲙⲁⲕⲁⲣⲓ: his designation as ⲉⲓⲱⲧ suggests that Makari(os) was a person of some consequence; cf. Barns, *Prel. Rep.* 14.

8 Perhaps ⲧⲓ/[ⲙⲟⲑⲉⲟⲥ; cf. line 17.
Verso
2 Probably ⲛ†]ⲙⲡϣⲁ [ⲁⲛ (cf. R 5).
2 f. may be tentatively translated as "I am not] worthy [of (an honor, aut sim.)] of this magnitude."
Address
6 f. We may possibly restore: [ⲧⲁⲁⲥ ⲙ]ⲡⲁⲡⲣ[ⲟ]ⲫⲏⲧ[ⲏⲥ] ⲛ̅ⲉⲓⲱⲧ [ⲡⲁϩⲱⲙⲉ ϩⲓⲧⲙ ⲡⲁⲡⲛⲟⲩ]ⲧⲉ, "deliver it to my prophet and father Pahome, from Papnoute." Mr. James Goehring has called our attention to the fact that Pachomius is frequently referred to as "our father, the prophet Apa Pachomius," in an Arabic text published by A. van Lantschoot, "Allocution de Timothée d'Alexandrie," *Le Muséon* 47 (1934) 13-56 (see, e.g., the opening section on p. 26). Further, the phrase ⲡⲁⲉⲓⲱⲧ ⲙⲡⲣⲟⲫⲏⲧⲏⲥ is regularly used by Besa in his *Life of Shenoute* as a designation of his master (J. Leipoldt, *Sinuthii vita bohairice* [*CSCO* Copt. 2.2]; see, e.g., 14.10).

7

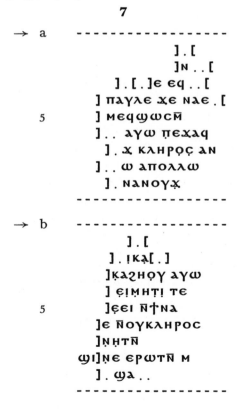

→ a   - - - - - - - - - - - - - - - - -
                    ] . [
                    ]ⲛ . . [
              ] . [.]ⲉ ⲉϥ . . [
          ] ⲡⲁⲩⲗⲉ ⲭⲉ ⲛⲁⲉ . [
5   ] ⲙⲉϥϣⲱⲥⲙ̅
          ] . . ⲁⲩⲱ ⲡⲉⲭⲁϥ
            ] . ⲭ ⲕⲗⲏⲣⲟⲥ̧ ⲁⲛ
          ] . . ⲱ ⲁⲡⲟⲗⲗⲱ
          ] . ⲛⲁⲛⲟⲩⲭ̧
          - - - - - - - - - - - - - - - - -

→ b   - - - - - - - - - - - - - - - - -
                  ] . [
              ] . ⲓⲕⲁ̧[.]
            ]ⲕⲁϩⲏⲟⲩ ⲁⲩⲱ
          ] ⲉ̧ⲓⲙⲏⲧ̧ⲓ ⲧⲉ
5   ]ⲉ̧ⲉⲓ ⲛ̅†ⲛⲁ
          ]ⲉ ⲛ̅ⲟⲩⲕⲗⲏⲣⲟⲥ
          ]ⲛ̧ⲏⲧⲛ̅
      ϣⲓ]ⲛ̧ⲉ ⲉⲣⲱⲧⲛ̅ ⲙ
          ] . ϣⲁ . .
          - - - - - - - - - - - - - - - - -

a 2 After ɴ possibly ϥ 3 Last letter є? 6 Before ⲁⲩⲱ probably
ⲁ or ⲗ 7 First letter ɪ? Apparently not ɴ]є.ⲝ 8 Before ⲱ possily ɪ
9 First letter ⲙ?
b 2 First letter ⲁ, ⲕ, or ⲗ? 4 ⲧɪ corrected

a

7 ⲕⲗⲏⲣⲟⳅ: the same word appears in b 6; in neither place is
its significance clear.

8 E.g. ⲁⲡⲟⲗⲗⲱ/[ɴɪⲟⳅ, or perhaps simply ⲁⲡⲟⲗⲗⲱ, complete in itself.

b

3 Possibly the expression ⲕⲱⲕ ⲁ2ⲏⲩ, "to strip."
8 Some final greetings: "I (?)] greet you."

Inv. VII 99ᶜ (see above, introduction to **6** and **7**)

```
        ------
  →     ]ⲣⲟ̣ɪ[
        ]єⲕ.[
        ------
```

(The verso is blank)

8 LETTER OF A MONK

Inv. VII 104ᶜ (a): 9 × 16 cm.; 101ᶜ (b): 5.2 × 1.7 cm.; 103ᶜ (c):
3.5 × 0.9 cm.; 105ᶜ (d): 2 × 0.2 cm.

In this papyrus the horizontal and vertical layers have mostly
become separated, and except for one large piece (a), the text as a
whole remains disintegrated. The names of both sender and addressee are illegible, but the former describes himself as a monk (see
the address on the verso); and of the community to which the letter
is addressed, one is ⲥⲁɴⳅɴⲱ(ⳅ) (a 16, b 2), possibly the individual
promiment elsewhere in this archive (but see above, Introd. 7).

Little of the text can be reconstructed beyond the customary
greetings in an unusually elaborate form, and any special message
it may have contained is lost. The writing is a clear, though in-
elegant semi-cursive; the orthography is rather poor.

```
  →  a  ---------------------------------
        [               ]ⲡ.ⲁ̣[
        [               ]ⳅⲟ̣...[
        [               ]6ɴⲛ̄ⲡϫⲟєɪ[ⳅ
        [ⲡⲙⲁɪɴⲟⲩⲧ]ⲉ̣ ɴⲛ̄ⲁⲅⲁⲑⲟⳅ ⲡɴⲁ[ⲏⲧ
```

5   [†]ϣⲓⲛ[ⲉ] ⲉⲡⲁⲓ̈ⲱⲧ ⲡⲁⲛⲉⲭⲁ[
    ⲛ̣ⲛⲡⲭⲟⲉⲓⲥ ⲡⲙⲁⲛⲟⲩⲧⲉ ⲛⲛ̄ⲁ[ⲅⲁⲑⲟⲥ]
    ⲡⲛ̣ⲁⲏⲧ †ϣⲓⲛⲉ ⲁⲡⲗⲁⲟ̣ⲥ̣ . [
    †ϣⲓⲛⲉ ⲛⲛ̄ⲥⲛⲏⲟⲩ ⲧⲏⲣ[ⲟ]ⲩ ⲁ̣[
    ⲉ̣ⲧⲟⲩⲣⲉⲓ[   ] . . ϭ̣[
10 . ⲙⲉ̣ⲩ . [   ] . . ⲛ[
    [. .] . . [   ]ⲍ̣ⲁ̣ . . [
    . . . . . . [   ]ϣⲁⲣⲁ . ⲛ̣[
    [.] . ⲛ[.] . [   ]ⲥⲟⲥ ⲁⲡⲡⲁ ⲥ̣ⲁ̣[
    ⲉⲧϥⲏ ⲟⲩϣⲏⲙ ⲉⲃⲣⲉ ϣⲉⲗⲃⲁ[ⲙ
15 ⲙⲛ̄ ⲟⲩϣⲏⲙ ⲉⲛⲉ̣ϥⲃⲣⲉ̣ . . . . [
    ⲡⲁⲉⲓⲱ̄ⲧ ⲥⲁⲛⲥⲛⲱ ⲡⲉⲧⲉⲃⲉ̣ . [
    ⲭⲣ . . . ⲙ̣ⲙ̣ⲟϥ ⲧ̄ⲛ̄ⲛⲁⲩ ⲛⲡ[
    ⲁⲩⲱ ⲧⲉⲧⲛ̣ⲥⲛ̣† ⲛⲉⲛⲡⲉⲧⲛ̄[
    ⲉⲟⲩⲭⲁⲓ ⲙⲙⲡⲭⲟⲉⲓⲥ̣   [

b   - - - - - - - - - - - - - - - - - -
    ] . ⲏⲓ . [
    ] . ⲁⲡⲡⲁ ⲥⲁⲛⲥⲛⲱ ⲣ[
    ]ⲛ̄ⲛⲛⲉϭ ϣⲗⲏⲁ̣[
    - - - - - - - - - - - - - - - - - -

c   - - - - - - - - - -
    ]ⲛ̄ⲧ̄ⲛⲏⲟⲩ . [
    ] . . ⲉ̣ⲙ . [
    - - - - - - - - - -

d   - - - - - - - - - -
    ]ⲡⲁⲥⲟⲛ . [
    - - - - - - - - - -

Verso   a

→   ⲧ]ⲉ̣ⲉⲥ ⲉⲙⲡⲁⲓⲱⲧ [   ] ⲡϣⲱ̣ⲥ̣ . . ϣ̣ϣⲟⲛ
                                        ϣⲁ̣ⲥ̣ⲉⲛⲏ ⲙⲟⲛⲟⲭⲟⲥ

a 2 ⲥⲟ̣ . . .: apparently not ⲥ̣ⲁ̣ⲛ̣ⲥ̣ⲛ̣[ⲱ   3 ⲙⲡⲭⲟⲉⲓⲥ? So also in
line 6 below   4 ⲛⲁⲅⲁⲑⲟⲥ, as in line 6   6 ⲡⲙⲁⲓⲛⲟⲩⲧⲉ   7 ⲉⲡⲗⲁⲟⲥ
8 ⲉⲛⲉⲥⲛⲏⲩ   12 Above ϣⲁⲣⲁ . ⲛ an illegible supralinear addition
13 Possibly ⲥⲁ̣[ⲛⲥⲛⲱ   14 ⲉⲧⲃⲉ (?); ⲉⲃⲣⲁ (ⲛ)ϣⲗϭⲟⲙ   15
ⲉⲛⲉϥⲃⲣⲉ̣: ⲛⲉⲃⲣⲁ   17 Possibly ⲭⲣⲓ̣ⲁ, followed by ϭ[ⲉ]   18
ⲧⲉⲧⲛⲥⲛⲧⲉ   19 ⲟⲩⲭⲁⲓ ϩⲙ ⲡⲭⲟⲉⲓⲥ
b 1 First letter probably ⲛ; last might be ⲣ   2 ⲁⲡⲁ   3 ⲛⲉⲭ
c 1 Last letter possibly ⲛ
    verso a ⲧⲁⲁⲥ ⲙⲡⲁⲉⲓⲱⲧ; after this a blot; there may well have been
a space before the name of the addressee   2 ⲙⲟⲛⲁⲭⲟⲥ

a

2   The line may well have begun [†ϣⲓⲛⲉ ⲉⲡⲁⲉⲓⲱ]ⲧ ⲥⲟ . . . [,
"I greet my father So---." But if so, the spacing seems to require
some further designation of the recipient at the beginning of the
next line.

3   Perhaps ⲡⲛⲟ]ϭ ⲛⲛⲡⲭⲟⲉⲓ[ⲥ (i.e. ⲙⲡⲭⲟⲉⲓⲥ), "the great
one of the Lord." Whatever the word may have been, it may have
followed ⲡⲁⲛⲉⲭⲁ[in line 5 as well.

4   (cf. 6 f.)   The expression ⲡⲙⲁⲓⲛⲟⲩⲧⲉ ⲛⲁⲅⲁⲑⲟⲥ ⲡⲛⲁⲏⲧ
is somewhat puzzling. At first sight it could appear to qualify the
person in each case: "the good, God-loving one, the compassionate."
ⲁⲅⲁⲑⲟⲥ, however, is generally an epithet of God himself; and
if ⲁⲅⲁⲑⲟⲥ and ⲛⲁⲏⲧ are applied to the same person, it is hard
to see why the writer should not have joined the epithets with the
attributive ⲛ. Possibly, therefore, the expression means "the lover
of the good God, the compassionate one."

5   ⲡⲁⲛⲉⲭⲁ[: the name ⲡⲁⲛⲉⲭⲁⲧⲏⲥ is not uncommon; see
NB and Onomasticon, s.v.

7   Perhaps restore ⲁⲡⲗⲁⲟ̣ⲥ ⲧ̣[ⲏⲣϥ ⲁⲩⲱ, "(I greet) all the
people and . . ."

9   Perhaps a relative clause.

14 f.   Although the reading of line 15 is by no means certain
after ⲉⲛⲉϥⲃⲣⲉ̣, it is not impossible that we have ⲉⲛⲉϥⲃⲣⲉ̣
ϣⲉ̣ⲗϭ[ⲁⲙ, a repetition in phonologically fuller form of ⲉⲃⲣⲉ
ϣⲉⲗϭⲁ[ⲙ in line 14.

In Prel. Rep. 15, this text was described as follows: "Another
Coptic letter seems to compare the growth of the particular community to which it was addressed to that of a grain of mustard
seed." This description was made before the piece was assembled in
its present form; formerly it was believed to contain the phrase
ⲁⲩⲥ̣ⲛ ⲧⲉⲧⲛⲥⲛ† ⲛⲑ[ⲉ ⲛⲟⲩϭⲣⲟϭ (?)] ⲙⲛ̄ ⲟⲩϣⲏⲙ ⲉⲛⲉϥⲃⲣⲉ̣
ϣⲉⲗϭ[ⲁⲙ, "your foundation has been set like a seed and a little
grain of mustard." What was then interpreted as ⲁⲩⲥ̣ⲛ ⲧⲉⲧⲛⲥⲛ†
ⲛⲑ[ⲉ has been shown to be misread, and the fragment to which
it belongs has been fixed as the beginning of line 18: ⲁⲩⲱ ⲧⲉⲧⲛⲥⲛ†
ⲛⲉⲛⲡⲉⲧⲛ[.

b

3   -ⲛⲉϭ ϣⲗⲏⲗ: cf. 4.23.

9-14 MISCELLANEOUS FRAGMENTS

We here give a transcription of some of the tiny Coptic fragments which are found in this cover but which we have not been able to identify. We include only the larger fragments or those which contain at least one identifiable word.

9

Inv. VII 111ᶜ: 4.7 × 2.8 cm.

(Upper margin?)

→ 　]... ⲱⲃⲉⲧⲟⲛ

　　]... ⲱⲃⲉⲧⲟⲛ

- - - - - - - - - - -

(The verso is blank)

10

Inv. VII 115ᶜ: 2.5 × 3.8 cm.

- - - - - - - - - - -

→ 　]ⲥⲁⲃⲱ[

- - - - - - - - - - -

(The verso is blank)

1]ⲥⲁⲃⲱ[: e.g. ⲧⲛⲁⲧ]/ⲥⲁⲃⲱ[ⲧⲛ, "I shall teach you."

11

Inv. VII 117ᶜ: 4 × 0.8 cm. (Which side preceded the other is unknown.)

a 　 - - - - - - - - - - - -

→ 　]ⲑⲉⲓⲁⲕⲁ[

- - - - - - - - - - -

b 　 - - - - - - - - - - -

→ 　]ⲥⲓ[

　]ⲛ[

(One line lost)

　] . [

　]ϭⲓ[

- - - - - - - - - - -

a

1 　]ⲑⲉⲓⲁⲕⲁ[: perhaps the personal name ⲑⲉⲕⲗⲁ?

12

Inv. VII 118ᶜ: 2.5 × 0.7 cm.

→   -----------
] . ϵ ⲛ ⲁ ⲓ ⲥ [

(On the verso: faint traces, perhaps of writing)

1   The demonstrative pronoun ⲚⲀⲒ may have been intended here.

13

Inv. VII 120ᶜ: 1.5 × 1.8 cm.

ⲁ ⲉ . [

(The verso is blank)

14

Inv. VII 126ᶜ: 1.6 × 1.7 cm.

] . ϵ . [
] ⲡ ⲁ ⲏ ⲥ [ϵ

(The verso is blank)

CODEX VIII

15 LETTER OF ISAAC, PSAI, AND BENJAMIN TO MESOUER(IS)

Inv. VIII 46ᶜ: 6.8 × 8.2 cm.

The hand is of an uncial type, and irregularity in size and shape shows that the writer is not very expert. Too little remains of the text to enable us to restore more than the opening formula or to judge the general standard of the orthography. The dialect seems to be standard Sahidic. The verso preserves no trace of an address.

```
     [ICA]AK M[N] ψAϊ MN̄ BEN[IAMIN NET]
     [CϨ]Aϊ M̄MECOYHP[(IC) XAIPE. ϨAθH N]
     [Ϩω]B NIM TN̄ϢINE [EPOK
     [. .]Ṇ ETNANOYϥ M̄[N
5    [.]ṆE N̄CNHY THPO[Y
     [N]ETϨAϨTHK E . [
     [.] MN̄ ΠMN̄ṬO[YE
     [.] NAK MN̄ . [
     [.]. MNT̂ . [
10   [.]ọOYCCE[
     [.]EP̣Ḥ[Y (?)
```
- -

It is Isaac, Psai, and Benjamin who write to Mesouer(is), greetings. Before everything we greet you ... who is (?) good and ... all the brothers ... who are with you ... and the eleven ... to you and ... each other (?) ...

1 ψAϊ: Ψάι(ς) is common in the papyri; see *NB* and *Onomasticon*, s.v.

2 MECOYHP[(IC): cf. Μεσουῆρις in *NB* and *Onomasticon*. The scribe may have written simply MECOYHP.

16 PRIVATE LETTER

Inv. VIII 41ᶜ (a): 3.5 × 10.5 cm.; 42ᶜ (b): 1.5 × 1.5 cm.; 43ᶜ (c): 3 × 1.5 cm.; 44ᶜ (d): 2.3 × 2.3 cm.; 45ᶜ (e): 3.5 × 3.1 cm.

Five fragments survive of this text. The first line of fragment a contains part of the standard epistolary formula. The relative position of b and c can be established by fiber correspondence with a, [1] but how much has been lost between the three pieces we cannot determine. Part of the left margin appears in a, and c preserves some of the right. Fragment d cannot be placed, but e, with its lower margin intact, represents the end of the letter, or at least the last part of a column. The hand is neat and practiced and bears strong resemblance to an early fourth-century book hand. Although too little remains to justify a translation, it is clear that this letter is written in standard Sahidic, with good orthography. The papyrus is extremely thin, and some of the writing on the recto has penetrated through to the verso.

The verso of the Greek text published as **143a** contains a mirror image of the first nine lines of fragment a.

```
→  a   - - - - - - - - - - - - - -
       ϩⲁⲑⲏ ⲛϩ[ⲱⲃ ⲛⲓⲙ
       ϯⲛⲟⲩ ϭ[ⲉ
       ⲙⲉⲉⲧⲁ[
       ⲛⲁⲥⲡ̄ϥⲉ[              b   - - - - - - - -
    5  ⲟⲩⲏⲡⲉ[                    ] . [      c   - - - - - - - - - -
       ⲉⲃⲱⲕ ⲛ̄[                  ]ⲙⲉⲛⲛ . [      ]ⲡⲱϩ ⲛⲥϩⲁⲓ
       ⲱⲁⲉⲓⲛ̄ⲣ . [               ]ⲧⲁϩⲉ[         ] . ⲧϥ̄ⲉⲗⲉⲓⲛ
       ⲟⲩⲱϣ[                     ]ⲁϩⲉⲟ[          ]ⲁⲗⲏⲑⲱⲥ
       ⲉⲣⲏⲩ[                      - - - - - - - -     - - - - - - - - - -
   10  [
       [ . . . ] . [
       ⲱⲕⲁⲛ . [
       ⲓⲙ̄ⲡⲓⲁ[
       ⲧⲁⲓ̈ⲥⲁϩ[
   15  ⲫⲩⲥⲓⲛ[
       ⲱ ϣⲧⲁⲁ[
       ⲙ̄ⲡⲉϥⲃⲉⲕ[ⲉ
       ⲛⲁⲓ̈ⲭ . [
       ⲃ . [
       - - - - - - - - - - - - - -
```

[1] On Pl. 67 of *The Facsimile Edition of the Nag Hammadi Codices: Cartonnage* (Leiden 1979), the position of the fragments must be slightly adjusted: 42ᶜ and 43ᶜ are to be moved up one line in respect to their alignment with 41ᶜ; see J. M. Robinson's remarks in his Preface, xxi.

d   - - - - - - - - - - - - -
         ] . ⲕϩ . . ⲁ[
         ]ⲱϣϥ ⲧⲟ[
         ]ⲉⲝⲟⲩⲱⲧ[
         ]ⲏⲥ ⲙⲛ̅[
5   ]ⲕ̣[
         - - - - - - - - - - - - -

e   - - - - - - - - - - - - -
         ]ⲣ . [.] . [
         ⲥⲛⲏ]ⲩ ⲧⲏⲣⲟⲩ ⲉ̣[
         ϣⲓ]ⲛ̣ⲉ ⲉⲣⲱⲧⲛ [

a

1 Probably the addressee and sender were named in the preceding line(s). After ϩⲁⲑⲏ ⲛ̅ϩ[ⲱⲃ ⲛⲓⲙ, restore ϯϣⲓⲛⲉ ⲉⲣⲱⲧⲛ
vel sim. (cf. e 3), "before everything I greet you."

13 The first letter appears to be iota with the left dot of a diaeresis.

e

3 ϣⲓ]ⲛ̣ⲉ: probably ϯϣⲓ]ⲛ̣ⲉ (cf. a 1), "I greet you."

17 PRIVATE LETTER

Inv. VIII 37ᶜ (a): 6 × 8.5 cm.; 38ᶜ (b): 3.8 × 5 cm.; 39ᶜ (c):
2.3 × 5.4 cm.; 40ᶜ (d): 3.2 × 6.8 cm.

This letter is preserved in four fragments, of which the first (a)
contains a greeting formula and doubtless came near the beginning;
it also displays part of the left margin. The position of the remaining
pieces cannot be established. No writing is visible on the versos.

→ a   - - - - - - - - - - -
           . ⲁⲧⲉ[
           ϯϣⲓⲛ[ⲉ
           ⲛⲅⲁⲣ ⲛ . [
           . . . ⲉ̣ⲡ[
5   ⲉⲡⲃ . . . [
           ⲛⲟⲭϣ[
           ⲣⲁ ϣ ⲉ[
           ⲛⲁ ⲕ . [
           . ⲉⲛ̣ . . [
10   . . [
           - - - - - - - - - - -

b

    ] Traces of 2 lines [
    ]ⲛⲡⲣⲉϩ[
    ] . ⲟⲟⲩϥⲙ . [
5   ]ⲩ[. .]ⲉ[.] . [

----

c

    ] . [
    ] . ⲛⲁ[
    ] . . ⲣⲁ[
    ]ⲏⲛ[
5   ] . . [
    ] . ⲧ . [
    ]ⲉ[

----

d

    ]ⲣⲁ[
    ]ϩⲟ[
    ] . . . ⲧ[
    ] . ⲡϩⲟϥ [
5   ]ⲃⲉⲗⲟⲕⲉ[
    ] . ⲉⲣⲫ[
    ] . ⲟ[
    ]ⲛ[
    ] . [

----

a

3 ⲛⲅⲁⲣ: i.e. γάρ; for the spelling, see, e.g., P. E. Kahle, *Bala'izah* (Oxford 1954) I 102.

18 PRIVATE LETTER

Inv. VIII 30ᶜ (a): 10.2 × 2.1 cm.; 31ᶜ (b): 3.5 × 1 cm.; 32ᶜ (c): 5.5 × 7.8 cm.; 33ᶜ (d): 1.9 × 6.8 cm.; 34ᶜ (e): 1.3 × 3.7 cm.; 35ᶜ (f): 1.5 × 2.7 cm.; 36ᶜ (g): 0.8 × 3.5 cm.

We publish here several scraps of what is evidently a private letter, although the first line (a 1) contains nothing recognizable as a personal name or intelligible as a formula of greeting. Fragment a bears the upper margin; we have not been able to establish the relative position of the other pieces. The writing is large and fairly fluent. There is part of a line of writing, probably an address, on the verso of e.

→ a]ϥ . . ογεεναειμαϛαραει[
‑‑‑‑‑‑‑‑‑‑‑‑‑‑‑‑‑‑‑‑‑‑‑

b ‑‑‑‑‑‑‑‑‑‑‑‑‑‑‑‑
]αγαπη[
] . [. .] . н[
‑‑‑‑‑‑‑‑‑‑‑‑‑‑

c ‑‑‑‑‑‑‑‑‑‑‑‑‑‑‑‑‑‑‑‑‑‑‑
κ]ατα ѳетн̣н[
] . ноγ мононн̣[
]τινογ τιϲϩ[αι
]αχετω . [
5]нϭ мπ̄ноγте ạ[
]γρε . [.] . [.]о . [
] . [   ]†ϩа[
          ]ϩ̄ π[
          ] . ειπ̄[
‑‑‑‑‑‑‑‑‑‑‑‑‑‑‑‑‑‑‑‑‑‑

d ‑‑‑‑‑‑‑‑‑
]ẹειχ[
]ογνạ[
]ωκạτ[
]неιм[
5] . . τιм[
‑‑‑‑‑‑‑‑

e ‑‑‑‑‑‑‑‑
] . . [
] . . [
]ет[
] . ạ[
‑‑‑‑‑‑‑‑

f ‑‑‑‑‑‑‑‑
] . ạτ[
]н ̄н[
]ϩ̣е[
‑‑‑‑‑‑‑‑

g   - - - - - - - -
       ]τ[
       - - - - - - - -

Verso e - - - - - - - - - - -
→   ] . . . oγ x[λ ι (?)

a 1 Perhaps]ϥ μ ε̣ o γ ε (i.e. ϥ μ ε ε γ ε) ε ν λ ε ι, "he is thinking of these"
9 First letter possibly κ
c 2 H corrected from ε ι
d 5 Perhaps ε]π̣ι̣τ ι μ[λ (ἐπιτιμᾶν)

19   PRIVATE LETTER (?)

Inv. VIII 58ᶜ (a): 7 × 2.5 cm.; 59ᶜ (b): 2 × 2.3 cm.

This text, perhaps a private letter, consists of two fragments; their relative position cannot be determined. The versos are blank.

a   - - - - - - - - - - -
           ] . [
     ]π̅π̅κλ2 [
     ]τ ϣ ω ω x ϣ[
     - - - - - - - - - - -

b   - - - - - - - - - - -
       ] . [
     ]x̣ι x ι . [
     ] . . . [
     - - - - - - - - - - -

INDEXES

N.B. 1) Except when we quote individual words, our method of citation does not differentiate between words actually read in the papyrus and those wholly or partially restored. 2) Only in the case of ambiguity is a translation given in the indices. 3) For No. **5** we employ our interpretative transcript and do not record the orthography of the diplomatic transcript.

I.   INDEX OF PROPER NAMES

II.   INDEX OF COPTIC WORDS

ⲕⲉ- **2** Y V 6; **4.12** (ⲕⲟ̣ⲩⲉ̣)
ⲕⲟⲩⲓ **5**.3
ⲕⲱ **2** X V 4; **4.**4, 9
ⲕⲱⲧⲉ **2** X R 12
ⲕⲁϩ **2** X R 30, Y R 10, 14; **19** a 2

ⲙⲁ **2** X V 7, Y R 1; **4.**26, 27
ⲙⲉ love **4.**18
    ⲙⲁⲓⲛⲟⲩⲧⲉ **8** a 4, 6 (ⲙⲁ-)
    ⲙⲉⲣⲓⲧ **4.**1, 20, 24; **6.**1 (ⲙⲉⲛⲡⲓⲧ), 5 (ⲙⲉⲛ̣ⲡⲓⲧ), 8
ⲙⲉ truth **2** X R 33
ⲙⲁⲁⲃ **2** X V 13
ⲙⲕⲁϩ **4.**6, 11
ⲙⲛ- with **2** X R 5, 7, 8, 16, 20, 34, V 35, 39, Y V 2; **3.**7; **4.**2, 23;
    5.2; **6.**11; **8** a 15; **15.**1, 4, 7, 8; **16** d 4
    ⲛⲙⲙⲁ⸗ **2** X R 17, 19, Y R 13; **4.**12 (ⲛⲉ̣ⲙⲙⲉ), 22 (ⲛⲙ̣ⲁⲕ);
        5.3
ⲙⲡϣⲁ **4.**9 (ⲙϣⲁ); **6.**5, V 2
ⲙⲟⲩⲣ
    ⲙⲣⲣⲉ **2** Y R 2 (ⲙⲉⲉ]ⲣⲉ; see note ad loc.)
ⲙⲓⲥⲉ
    ⲙⲁⲥⲉ **2** X V 16
ⲙⲏⲧ **2** X V 15, 16; **5.**7
    ⲙⲛⲧ- **15.**9 (ⲙⲛⲧ.[)
    ⲙⲛⲧⲟⲩⲉ **15.**7
ⲙⲁⲧⲉ greatly
    ⲉⲙⲁⲧⲉ **2** X R 18; **4.**6, 14
ⲙⲏⲧⲉ **2** X V 22
ⲙⲧⲟ **2** X R 12
ⲙⲧⲟⲛ **4.**17 (ⲙⲙⲧⲟⲛ)
ⲙⲁⲩ
    ⲉⲧⲙⲙⲁⲩ **2** X V 8
ⲙⲁⲁⲩ **2** X V 1
ⲙⲁⲩⲁⲁ⸗ **2** X V 19
ⲙⲟⲩⲟⲩⲧ **2** Y V 10
ⲙⲟⲟϣⲉ **2** X V 20 (ⲙⲟϣⲉ), 29 (ⲙⲟϣⲉ)
ⲙⲟⲩϩ fill
    ⲙⲉϩⲥⲛⲧⲉ **2** X R 24
    ⲙⲉϩⲥⲛⲁⲩ **2** X V 35 (ⲙⲉⲩ-)
    ⲙⲉϩϣⲟⲙⲛⲧ **2** X V 36

ⲧⲱⲕ be strong **4**.14, 21
ⲧⲁⲙⲟ **4**.16
ⲧⲱⲙⲧ meet **2** X R 16 (ⲧⲱⲙⲛⲧ), V 25, 40
ⲧⲱⲛ where?
    ⲉⲧⲱⲛ **2** X V 28
ⲧⲛⲛⲟⲟⲩ **2** X R 9, V 32; **5**.5
ⲧⲏⲣ⸗ **2** Y V 8; **4**.3, 5; **8** a 8; **15**.5; **16** e 2
ⲧⲱⲣⲉ
    ⲉⲧⲟⲟⲧ⸗ **2** X R 1, V 23, 34
    ⲛⲧⲟⲟⲧ⸗ **5**.7
    ϩⲓⲧⲛ- **2** X V 17
ⲧⲥⲛⲕⲟ **2** X V 14
ⲧⲱⲧ **4**.26
ⲧⲟⲟⲩ buy **5**.4
ⲧⲟⲩⲛⲟⲥ **4**.20
ⲧⲟⲩϫⲟ **2** X R 38
ⲑⲃⲃⲓⲟ **3**.3 (ⲑⲃⲃⲓⲏⲩ)
ⲧⲁϫⲣⲟ **4**.26

ⲟⲩ- ϩⲉⲛ- indefin. art., passim
ⲟⲩ what? **2** Y R 8; **5**.9
ⲟⲩⲁ one
    ⲟⲩⲁ ⲟⲩⲁ **4**.3
    ⲙⲛⲧⲟⲩⲉ **15**.7
ⲟⲩⲱ news **2** X R 10; **4**.12, 13, 15
ⲟⲩⲟⲛ some **2** X V 36
ⲟⲩⲛⲟⲩ
    ⲧⲛⲟⲩ **2** X R 36; **16** a 2; **18** c 3 (ⲧⲓⲛⲟⲩ)
    ⲧⲉⲛⲟⲩ **4**.4, 13, 15, 24
ⲟⲩⲱϣ wish **3**.4 (ⲟⲩⲱϣⲉ); **4**.15 (ⲟⲩⲱϣⲉ); **16** a 8
ⲟⲩϣⲏ
    ⲛⲧⲉⲩϣⲏ **2** X V 8
ⲟⲩⲱϩ **2** X R 5, V 33, 37, Y R 1
ⲟⲩϫⲁⲓ vb. **2** X R 25 (ⲟⲩⲟⲟϫ)
    nn. **8** a 19 (ⲉⲟⲩϫⲁⲓ; sic); **18** e V 1 (?)

ⲱ **3**.4
ⲱⲛϩ **4**.28; **5**.10
ⲱⲡ **2** X V 6, 27
    ⲏⲡⲉ **16** a 5 (?)

ⲱⲥⲕ **2** X R 6
ⲱϩⲉ ⲉⲣⲁⲧ⸗ **4**.21

ϣⲁ- **2** X R 13, 14, Y R 9
   ϣⲁⲣⲟ⸗ **2** Y V 12, 14
   See also ϩⲣⲁⲓ
ϣⲉ hundred **2** X R 17
ϣⲱ **2** X V 5
ϣⲗⲏⲗ **4**.23, 25; **8** b 3
ϣⲗϭⲟⲙ **8** a 14 (ϣⲉⲗϭⲁ[ⲙ])
ϣⲏⲙ **8** a 14, 15
ϣⲟⲙⲛⲧ **2** X V 36 (ϣⲟⲙⲧ)
ϣⲓⲛⲉ **4**.2, 11, 14; **5**.2; **6**.3, 4, 6; **7** b 8; **8** a 5, 7, 8; **15**.3; **16** e 3;
   17 a 2
   ϥⲁⲓϣⲓⲛⲉ **2** X R 13
ϣⲱⲛⲉ vb. **4**.5; **5**.6
   nn. **4**.6
ϣⲱⲡ **4**.19 (ϣⲟⲟⲡⲟⲩⲓ, i.e. ϣⲟⲡⲟⲩ)
ϣⲱⲡⲉ **2** X R 6, 24, Y R 11, V 5, 6; **3**.5; **4**.3, 23, 27; **5**.9
ϣⲏⲣⲉ **2** X V 2, 15, Y V 11, 14; **4**.19
   ⲁⲧϣⲏⲣⲉ **2** Y V 5
ϣⲱⲣⲡ
   ϣⲟⲣⲡ **2** X R 23, V 24, 35
ϣⲏⲧ **2** X V 11, 12
ϣⲧⲟⲣⲧⲣ **2** Y R 7
ϣⲁⲩ profit **4**.13
ϣⲁϫⲉ vb. **2** X V 39, Y R 13
   nn. **2** X V 38, Y R 14

ϥⲓ
   ϥⲁⲓϣⲓⲛⲉ **2** X R 13
ϥⲧⲟⲟⲩ
   ϥⲧⲉⲩ- **2** X R 16
   ϫⲟⲩⲧⲁϥⲧⲉ **5**.6

ϩⲁ- See ϩⲏ, ϩⲏⲧ
ϩⲉ fall **2** X R 11
ϩⲉ way
   ⲛⲑⲉ **2** X V 5

III. INDEX OF GREEK WORDS